The Use-It-Up Cookbook

The Use-It-Up Cookbook

A GUIDE TO USING UP PERISHABLE FOODS

Lois Carlson Willand

CHARLES SCRIBNER'S SONS / NEW YORK

Library of Congress Cataloging in Publication Data

Willand, Lois.
   The use-it-up cookbook.

   Includes index.
   1. Cookery (Leftovers)   I. Title.
TX740.W548   641.5'52   78-23918
ISBN 0-684-15888-4

1 3 5 7 9 11 13 15 17 19 O/C 20 18 16 14 12 10 8 6 4 2

Printed in the United States of America

Contents

Preface

For generations thrifty and clever cooks have devised numerous ways to prepare appealing meals from the food they had on hand. Successful ideas were shared with family and friends, mostly by word of mouth. A wealth of ideas and recipes thus existed, but scattered among countless cooks.

As one who wanted to be a thrifty but successful cook, I began to collect and write down ideas for preparing and serving foods. To help find those ideas quickly I filed the suggestions and recipes by the food to be used rather than by the final product, such as salad, main dish, or dessert.

Some of the recipes I found were similar in most respects but were varied in the amount of seasonings or leavening used. These recipes have been printed with variations and are labeled "As-You-Like-It" recipes. Another type of recipe was one that was helpful for using up many different kinds of food at the same time. These recipes are called "Use-It-Up" recipes; you will find them especially convenient when you have several foods that need to be used up quickly.

This book could not have been compiled without the sharing of ideas by good cooks of years past as well as by present-day cooks, including many friends, relatives, and neighbors who have contributed favorite recipes and ideas. All recipes have been tested in homes by homemakers and their families. Only recipes that passed the strict taste tests of children and adults and those that met the budget standards of thrifty cooks have been included.

I am especially grateful to Verna Mikesh, Professor Emeritus and Extension Nutritionist, Agricultural Extension Service, University of Minnesota, for her professional advice and encouragement. Special thanks go to Isabel D. Wolf, Extension Food and Nutrition Specialist, University of Minnesota, for providing information and advice on safe storage of perishable foods; and to Mary E. Darling, Extension Nutritionist, University of Minnesota, for information on metric measurement. Thanks also to my friends Alice Benjamin Boudreau, Margot Kriel, Shirley Levitt, Susan Anderson, and Judy Sawyer for their special interest and willingness to share ideas and reactions to this book as it grew into final form. And a fond thanks to my husband Jon and daughter Tona, who patiently ate the results of recipe testing for two years.

This book will bring you an accumulation of creative cooking ideas from the past and present. May those of you who use this book find help in planning and preparing meals and in developing creative food uses for your eating pleasure.

How to Use This Book

WHAT IS USE-IT-UP COOKING?

You may already cook the Use-It-Up way, at least part of the time. When you open the refrigerator door to see what's there to prepare and eat—that's Use-It-Up cooking. It's finding ways to use the half can of water chestnuts, the leftover vegetables, the raw egg yolks, the ever-mounting heap of zucchini or cucumbers from the garden, the sack of windfall apples, or the cranberries or turkey from Thanksgiving dinner.

Use-It-Up cooking—finding ways to eat up foods before they spoil—needs a quick and easy system for finding appropriate recipes. Cookbooks are filled with recipes that use up foods, but it is often difficult to find quickly all the recipes that include the food one wishes to use up. Here is how the *Use-It-Up Cookbook* offers a unique solution to that problem: the *Use-It-Up Cookbook*'s index, the most valuable part of this book, helps you find all the recipes or suggestions for utilizing the foods you need to use up. It works this way: in the *Use-It-Up Cookbook* index, look up the name of the food you want to use up (such as cottage cheese, rhubarb, roast beef, and so on). For each food there is a "How to Use" section which lists a variety of ideas on how to make use of the food. This is followed by a selection of titles of recipes that use that food. Finally, the "see also" references tell you what other recipes in the book include that food as part of their ingredients. By utilizing the Use-It-Up index you can quickly find dozens of suggestions for making use of a certain food in a variety of appealing ways. Let the Use-It-Up index be your indispensable guide whenever you need help on deciding how to use up a food.

THREE RULES OF USE-IT-UP COOKING

Use-It-Up cooking relies on three basic rules to make it a safe, efficient, and worthwhile system:

1. Store foods correctly and use promptly. More than one person has made an unexpected trip to a hospital because of food poisoning from improperly stored foods. Use-It-Up cooking requires that one store foods properly at the correct temperature, under sanitary conditions, and that the food be used within a safe time period. Perishable fresh foods should be refrigerated as soon as possible. Cooked foods should not be allowed to cool to room temperature but should be placed in clean, covered containers and refrigerated immediately after a meal. Partially used foods from cans should preferably be transferred to clean, covered glass or plastic containers rather than being stored in the can. As a general rule of thumb, use perishable foods within two or three days. If you suspect a food may be too old to use safely, *do not taste the food* but go by this rule: "When in doubt, throw it out!" See "Storage Guide for Perishable Foods" (page 166) for detailed instructions on safe storage of foods.

2. Keep track of which foods need to be used. Develop your own system, but get a system and stick with it. Your system must include a means of seeing at a glance which foods need using up. Setting aside a shelf or section of the refrigerator for perishables and leftovers is one way. Storing all perishables in see-through containers reminds you of their presence each time you open the refrigerator. Keeping a running list of leftovers and dates by which they must be used on the refrigerator door helps. Make a daily survey of which foods need to be used. Some people plan the use of leftovers as the food is used for the first time. And of course, written menu plans are probably the most foolproof method of making sure a food gets used during its safe-storage time.

3. Decide if the leftover or perishable food is really worth using. It's no secret that huge amounts of usable food are thrown into the garbage daily. Yet common sense tells us to consider our time, energy, and money. If we have to buy some expensive ingredient to prepare a dish that uses up 20 cents' worth of leftover food, or if we spend an hour or more of food preparation time on some inexpensive food item, or if we spend energy to fix an appealing dish from a food that has lost most of its nutrient value, then we have reached a point at which our use of time or resources exceeds the value of what we have prepared. Each person must set a standard of what is reasonable in terms of time, energy, and the cost of ingredients.

ADVANTAGES OF USE-IT-UP COOKING

The most obvious benefit to the user is the freedom one has to acquire supplies of food when they are available, knowing there will be numerous ways to utilize the food. One need not be afraid of purchasing a large amount of food when finding a good buy at the market, or of harvesting bumper garden crops or accepting an offering from a neighbor's garden bounty. Use-It-Up cooking allows you to buy, harvest, or accept foods in quantity whenever you have the opportunity to do so. Use-It-Up cooking also allows you to prepare special dishes knowing you will have a variety of ways to use leftover ingredients. Most important, your time devoted to menu planning can be used more efficiently with the help of the *Use-It-Up Cookbook*'s invaluable index. So shop, plan, cook, and eat with ease—and happy Use-It-Up cooking!

Bread, Grains, and Pasta

BREAD, STALE

How to Use: Toast and cube for croutons.

Dip in egg and milk mixture and fry for French toast.

Cut into attractive shapes; spread with garlic butter and bake at 350° for 10 to 25 minutes until crisp.

Dry and crumble for crumb toppings or bread crumb coatings.

Use in stuffings for poultry and meat.

Use for dipping in Swiss-type fondues or in baked fondues.

Crumble and add to ground meat dishes as an extender.

Use two slices of bread to thicken two cups of gravy.

Add to cooked turnips and rutabagas.

Use for bread puddings, Apple Brown Betty, crumb puddings.

Toast: Use for croutons or as thickening for soups and gravies.

Plain buns and rolls: Make dry bread crumbs.

BREAD CRUMBS

Dry bread crumbs: Dry bread in a 250° oven until thoroughly dry. Then whir in blender or place in a plastic bag and crush with a rolling pin. Store in an airtight container.

Browned bread crumbs: Brown dry crumbs in skillet over moderate heat, using ⅓ cup butter plus ½ teaspoon salt for each cup of bread crumbs. Use at once.

Soft bread crumbs: Use two- to four-day-old bread. Gently break bread apart with fork. Do not press down or pack crumbs. Use at once.

Seasoned bread crumbs: Use dry bread crumbs. Mix 1 teaspoon crushed oregano leaves, ½ teaspoon ground thyme, ½ teaspoon onion salt, ½ teaspoon salt, and ¼ teaspoon ground pepper to each cup of crumbs. Use to coat chicken, chops, and so on, before baking or frying.

CROUTONS

Cut dry bread or buttered toast into cubes. Toast in 250° oven until brown. For garlic croutons, heat a clove of crushed garlic in vegetable oil; remove garlic and pour oil over bread cubes. Toast in moderate oven until golden brown. Croutons may be frozen in plastic bags and recrisped in 350° oven 10 minutes. Use in soups and salads.

TOAST CUPS

Use one slice of bread for each cup. Trim crusts from bread; flatten bread with rolling pin and spread with butter. Press into a greased muffin cup and bake at 375° until golden brown, about 10 minutes. Use as pastry shells to hold creamed foods.

TOAST STICKS

Cut stale bread into sticks. Spread all sides with seasoned butter or margarine. Place on cookie sheet in 400° oven for 7 to 8 minutes, turning occasionally to toast all sides. Crisp under broiler if desired. Possible seasonings: garlic salt, oregano, dill weed, and garlic powder; or cinnamon and sugar.

Bread may be toasted first and then buttered and dipped in seasonings or grated Parmesan cheese.

CRUMBS, CRACKER

How to Use: Crush to same consistency with rolling pin. Store in tightly covered container in cool dry place.

Use crumbs in place of dry bread crumbs, cereal crumbs, or crumbled potato or corn chips as topping for casseroles.

Substitute for bread as binder for meat loaf or meat balls.

Substitute for dry bread crumbs as breading for foods to be fried.

Seasoned breading mix: Combine 1 cup cracker crumbs with 1 teaspoon salt, ¼ teaspoon pepper, and ½ teaspoon dried herbs of choice.

CRUMBS, CAKE AND COOKIE

How to Use: To make sweet crumbs, break cake or cookies into small pieces. If not crisp, place on baking sheet in oven at 250° until crumbs are dry.

Whirl in blender, or place in heavy plastic bag and crush with rolling pin. Store crumbs in tightly covered container in a cool dry place. Cake and cookie crumbs may be stored together.

Sprinkle sweet crumbs over puddings, Brown Betty, or cooked fruit.

Crumb pie shell: Blend 1½ cups sweet crumbs, ⅓ cup melted butter, and 3 tablespoons sugar. Press into a 9-inch pie pan. If desired, save one-third of the mixture as topping. Bake crust at 350° for 15 minutes; cool before adding filling. For an 8-inch pan, use 1¼ cups crumbs, 2 tablespoons sugar, and ¼ cup melted butter.

CRUMB COOKIES

2 cups cake or cookie crumbs
½ cup milk
¼ cup shortening
¼ cup peanut butter
½ cup brown sugar
1 egg
1 cup flour
½ teaspoon salt
1 teaspoon baking powder
¼ teaspoon baking soda
½ cup chopped nuts or raisins

In small bowl combine crumbs and milk; set aside. Cream shortening, peanut butter, sugar, and egg in large bowl. Sift dry ingredients and stir into egg mixture alternately with the crumb-milk mixture. Add nuts or raisins. Drop by teaspoonfuls onto a greased cookie sheet. Bake at 350° 15 minutes. Makes 3 dozen cakelike cookies.

CAKE, DRY

How to Use: Dry in oven to make sweet crumbs.

Break up into chunks and fold into whipped cream. Fold in a

dessert sauce such as custard, lemon or orange, chocolate, and so on. Chill several hours before serving. Serve in dessert bowls.

TRIFLE

> Dry cake such as angel food, yellow, white or sponge
> 2 to 6 tablespoons rum or sherry
> ½ cup jam or 1 to 2 cups sweetened fruit (reserve some fruit for garnish)
> 2 cups Soft Custard Sauce
> 1 cup whipped cream or whipped topping

Break or cut cake into 2-inch sections. Place cake in bottom of deep serving dish; sprinkle with rum or sherry. Spread cake with jam or fruit. Cover with Soft Custard Sauce (page 58). At this point, dessert may be chilled for several hours. Before serving, decorate with whipped cream or topping and garnish with fruit. Serves 4 to 6.

FRUIT CAKE COOKIES

> 1 stick (½ cup) margarine
> 1 cup brown sugar
> 1 egg
> 1 cup flour
> ½ teaspoon baking powder
> ¼ teaspoon salt
> 1 cup quick-cooking rolled oats
> 1½ cups fruit cake, crumbled

In large bowl cream together margarine and brown sugar until light and fluffy. Add egg and beat. Sift together flour, baking powder, and salt. Add to creamed mixture. Stir in rolled oats and fruit cake. Drop by teaspoonfuls 2 inches apart on well-greased baking sheet. Bake at 350° 8 to 10 minutes. Makes about 3 dozen cookies.

PASTA

How to Use: Freeze in freezer containers. When needed, thaw in covered container at room temperature, or run hot water over pasta, or place in boiling water only long enough to warm through.

Serve under sauces of meat with gravy, tomato sauce and meat, cheese sauce, or white sauce with meat and vegetables.

Place cooked pasta in greased baking dish; layer with cooked diced meat or seafood, grated cheese, mushrooms, diced celery, and green pepper, or whatever vegetables are desired. Salt and pepper to taste. Moisten with white sauce or gravy. Bake at 350° for 35 to 45 minutes.

Noodles: Use as base for Beef Stroganoff, Beef Burgundy, or goulash.

Macaroni: Use in goulash, macaroni and cheese, in meat or seafood salads, or add to soups.

Spaghetti: Use under tomato or cheese sauces, in tetrazzini dishes, or add to soups.

RICE

How to Use: Add milk, honey or brown sugar, and raisins for a breakfast dish.

Add to soup.

Use as base for cooked meat or poultry heated in a gravy or seasoned sauce, for chop suey base.

Use as extender for hamburger and meat loaf.

Use in croquettes or fritters.

Rice stuffing for meat or poultry: Combine rice, sautéed onion, and celery with seasonings and herbs such as sage, thyme, and so forth.

Use as base for a meat, vegetable, or fruit salad.

Rice and Bean Salad: Combine cooked rice, cooked kidney beans, chopped hard-cooked egg, sweet pickle relish, chopped onions, celery, and green pepper. Season to taste. Moisten with mayonnaise. Chill before serving.

Rice au Gratin: Place rice in greased baking dish; cover with cheese sauce and top with grated cheese. Bake at 350° for 20 minutes.

Brown rice: Use interchangeably with white rice in most recipes. Raw brown rice needs to be cooked 50 minutes or until tender.

RICE SALAD

2 cups cooked meat or fish, cubed
3 cups cooked rice
Any combination of vegetables:
½ cup celery, chopped
¼ cup radishes, sliced
¼ cup green pepper, chopped
¼ cup pitted olives, quartered
½ cup cooked peas
½ cup cucumber, peeled and sliced
2 tablespoons green onions, minced
¼ cup water chestnuts, sliced
½ cup parsley, chopped
2 tablespoons canned pimiento

Dressing:
½ cup vegetable oil
1 clove garlic, mashed
Pinch of thyme or basil, if desired
2 tablespoons white wine vinegar or tarragon vinegar
Tomato quarters or hard-cooked eggs for garnish
Lettuce leaves

In large bowl combine the garlic, oil, herbs, and vinegar. Add meat or fish; toss to coat. Stir in vegetables. Add rice and toss mixture gently to coat all rice grains. Chill until ready to serve. Garnish as desired before serving on lettuce leaves. Serves 6.

FRIED RICE

2 tablespoons vegetable oil
1 small onion, chopped, or 2 green onions
Canned mushrooms, if desired
½ cup water chestnuts, sliced
¼ cup parsley
3 cups cooked rice
Salt to taste
1 to 2 cups cooked meat, chopped
1 to 2 cups chopped cooked vegetables, if desired
2 tablespoons soy sauce
Dash pepper and ginger
½ teaspoon sugar
2 to 3 eggs, beaten

In medium skillet cook onion quickly in oil. Reduce heat and add mushrooms, water chestnuts, and parsley. Add rice, seasonings, meat, and vegetables; stir until heated. Make a well in center of the mixture; pour eggs into well. When eggs are half-cooked, blend them into the rice mixture. Serves 3 to 5.

GREEN RICE

2 *cups rice, cooked*
1 *cup milk*
1 *egg, beaten*
¼ to ½ *cup parsley, minced*
1 *small onion, minced*
½ *cup sharp cheese, grated*
1 *cup broccoli or spinach, chopped, cooked, and drained*
1 *teaspoon Worcestershire sauce*
  Garlic salt to taste

In large bowl beat egg. Add remaining ingredients and mix well. Pour into greased 1½-quart casserole. Bake at 325° 30 to 40 minutes. Serves 4.

HOPPING JOHN

2 *cups ham broth*
3 *cups black-eyed peas, cooked, or 3 cups cooked dried beans*
1 *cup cooked ham, cubed*
1 *cup white or brown rice, cooked*
3 *tablespoons parsley, minced*

In medium saucepan combine all ingredients. Heat thoroughly. Serves 6.

CHILI RICE WITH PEPPERS

1 *cup green peppers, chopped*
1 *cup onions, chopped*
1 *clove garlic, minced*
2 *tablespoons vegetable oil*
3 *cups rice, cooked*
1 *(16-ounce) can tomatoes*
1 *tablespoon chili powder*
1 *teaspoon salt*
1 *pound ground beef, sautéed and drained*
2 *cups kidney beans, drained*

In large skillet sauté green peppers, onions, and garlic in oil. Stir in rice, tomatoes, seasonings, ground beef, and beans. Heat thoroughly in skillet, or sprinkle with grated cheddar cheese or corn chips and heat 30 minutes in a 350° oven. Serves 4 to 6.

SPANISH RICE

>   2 *to 3 cups cooked rice*
>   4 *tablespoons vegetable oil*
>   1 *medium onion, minced*
>   1 *green pepper, minced*
>   ¼ *cup celery, diced*
>   2 *cups cooked tomatoes*
>   2 *teaspoons salt*
>   ⅛ *teaspoon pepper*
>   6 *slices bacon, fried, drained, and crumbled*

In medium skillet cook onion, green pepper, and celery in oil until onion is yellow. Add tomatoes, salt, and pepper and simmer 15 minutes. Stir in rice; heat 5 minutes. Serve topped with crumbled bacon. Serves 4 to 6.

RICE CRUST

>   2½ *cups cooked rice*
>   2 *eggs, beaten*
>   4 *tablespoons butter, melted*
>   ⅛ *teaspoon pepper*

In medium bowl combine all ingredients. Mix thoroughly. Press firmly into ungreased 9-inch pie pan. Fill with desired filling of meat, vegetables, or cheese in white sauce. Bake at 350° 40 minutes.

HEAVENLY RICE

>   1½ *cups cooked rice*
>   1 *cup fresh or canned fruit, diced*
>   ½ *cup whole cranberry sauce*
>   1 *banana, sliced*
>   ¼ *cup nuts, coarsely chopped*
>   1 *cup whipped topping*
>   *Sugar to taste*

In medium bowl with cover, mix fruits, nuts, and rice. Fold in whipped topping. Add sugar to taste. Chill 1 hour before serving. Garnish with sliced fruit, if desired. Serves 4.

RICE PUDDING

>   2 *large eggs or 4 egg yolks*
>   ½ *cup sugar*
>   ¼ *teaspoon salt*
>   2 *cups milk*
>   *Dash nutmeg*
>   1 *teaspoon vanilla*
>   2 *cups rice, cooked*
>   ½ *cup raisins*

In large bowl beat eggs, sugar, and salt together just enough to blend. Add milk, vanilla, nutmeg, rice, and raisins. Pour into greased 1-quart baking dish. Set in pan of water 1 inch deep. Bake at 325° 1 hour or until center is gently firm. Serves 6.

Dairy Products

BUTTERMILK

How to Use: Substitute in recipes calling for sour milk. Use same amount of buttermilk as sour milk.

Buttermilk may be substituted for sweet milk in some bread or cake recipes by substituting an equal amount of buttermilk for sweet milk, reducing the amount of baking powder or omitting it, and increasing the amount of baking soda by ½ to 1 teaspoon.

To freeze buttermilk, measure by ¼ cups into muffin tins and freeze. When frozen, loosen and store in a plastic bag in freezer. Thaw at room temperature or in a pan over very low heat.

Many recipes for muffins, biscuits, pancakes, waffles, doughnuts, and coffeecakes call for buttermilk.

Mix with brown sugar to form a thick sauce; use over hot cereal.

Substitute for oil in homemade salad dressings to make them lower in calories.

Use in spice cakes, devil's food cakes, banana cakes, German chocolate cakes.

Mix with applesauce and serve as sauce over corn bread or spice cake.

Add to cooked rice along with brown sugar, raisins, and nuts to make an instant rice pudding.

Buttermilk Cooler: Mix buttermilk with fruit such as orange, lemon, banana, or pineapple. Add honey or sugar to taste. Whirl in blender. If desired add raw egg and ice. Blend until mixture is foamy.

Chicken baked in buttermilk: Dip chicken pieces in buttermilk, then in seasoned flour. Melt ¼ cup butter or margarine in a baking dish; place chicken in baking dish skin side down. Bake, uncovered, at 375° for 30 minutes. Turn and bake 15 minutes more. Blend 1 cup buttermilk with a can of condensed cream of chicken soup; pour mixture around chicken and bake 15 minutes more or until done.

BUTTERMILK PANCAKES

1¼ cups flour
¾ teaspoon baking soda
1 tablespoon sugar
½ teaspoon salt
1 egg, slightly beaten
1¼ to 1½ cups buttermilk
¼ cup butter or margarine, melted

In medium bowl mix flour, baking soda, sugar, and salt. In separate bowl combine egg, buttermilk, and butter; mix well. Add milk mixture to dry ingredients and stir just until moistened. (Batter should be lumpy.) Spoon batter into lightly greased heated skillet. Cook until covered with bubbles and brown on the bottom; turn and brown the other side. Makes 8 to 10 large pancakes.

BUTTERMILK BEEF STROGANOFF

3 pounds lean beef
½ cup flour
2 teaspoons salt
¼ teaspoon pepper
¼ cup vegetable oil
2 cups onions, sliced
1 clove garlic, minced
1½ tablespoons Worcestershire sauce
¼ cup catsup
1 cup canned mushrooms (reserve liquid)
1½ cups buttermilk
Cooked noodles or rice

Cut meat in ½-by-2-inch strips. Combine flour, salt, and pepper; coat meat with flour mixture. In large skillet with cover or in Dutch oven, brown meat slowly in oil. Add onion, garlic, Worcestershire, and catsup. Add mushroom liquid plus enough water to make 1 cup; add to meat, cover, and simmer 2 to 2½ hours or until tender. Add additional water as needed (the mixture will be thick when meat is tender). Add mushrooms and buttermilk; cook over low heat only until heated through. Serve over rice or noodles. Serves 8 to 10.

BUTTERMILK POT ROAST

>   3- *to 4-pound beef pot roast*
>   2 *tablespoons flour*
>   1 *tablespoon dry mustard*
> 1½ *teaspoons salt*
>   ¼ *teaspoon pepper*
>   2 *tablespoons vegetable oil*
>   1 *beef bouillon cube*
>   ⅓ *cup water*
>   ½ *cup buttermilk*
>   6 *medium carrots, cut in 2-inch pieces*
> 1¼ *to 2 cups Brussels sprouts*
>   1 *cup buttermilk*
>   1 *to 2 tablespoons flour for thickening*

Combine flour, mustard, salt, and pepper; dredge meat with mixture. In large skillet with cover or in Dutch oven, brown meat in oil. Pour off excess drippings. Add beef bouillon cube and water to skillet; heat and stir to dissolve bouillon cube. Cover and cook over medium heat for 2 hours; add more water as necessary. Add ½ cup buttermilk, carrots, and Brussels sprouts; cover and cook for 30 minutes or until meat and vegetables are tender. Remove meat and vegetables to heated platter. Blend 1 cup buttermilk with flour and use to thicken cooking liquid for gravy. Serves 4 to 6.

BUTTERMILK POTATOES

> 2 *tablespoons butter*
> 2 *cups raw potatoes, peeled and chopped*
> ½ *teaspoon salt*
> ⅛ *teaspoon pepper*
> 1 *cup buttermilk*
>   *Paprika, if desired*

In large skillet melt butter and add potatoes. Cook over moderate heat, stirring frequently, until potatoes are lightly browned. Add salt, pepper, and buttermilk. Simmer uncovered until potatoes are tender and liquid is thickened, about 10 minutes. Sprinkle with paprika before serving, if desired. Serves 4.

BUTTERMILK CUSTARD PIE

1 *unbaked pastry or crumb pie shell*
3 *eggs, slightly beaten*
1½ *cups sugar*
¼ *cup butter or margarine, melted*
3 *tablespoons flour*
1 *teaspoon vanilla*
1 *teaspoon cinnamon*
1 *tablespoon vinegar, if desired*
¾ *cup buttermilk*

In medium bowl blend together eggs, sugar, butter, flour, vanilla, and cinnamon. Stir in vinegar and buttermilk. Pour into pie shell. Bake at 425° for 10 minutes, then reduce heat to 350° and bake until done, about 20 to 25 minutes more. Cool on rack; chill. Serve with fresh berries or peaches, if desired.

CHEESE

CHEESE, GENERAL

How to Use: Slice and use in broiled or grilled cheese sandwiches.
Grate and add to soups, salad dressings, use as topping for casseroles, hamburgers, potatoes, and vegetables. Grated cheese can be stored in airtight freezer containers until needed.
Use to make rarebits, fondues, soufflés, quiches, cheese sauces.
Dice and add to scrambled eggs and omelets, macaroni and cheese, cooked vegetables, vegetable-gelatin salads.
Add to pizza, lasagna, enchiladas, refried beans.
Freeze small chunks of cheese. Thaw at room temperature. Use for cooked dishes, as many cheeses become crumbly after thawing.
Slice and serve with crackers as appetizers, or with fresh fruit for dessert.

WINE-CHEESE SPREAD

½ *cup butter, softened*
2 *to 3 cups assorted cheese, grated*
Chopped pimiento or green olives, if desired

3 *tablespoons brandy, sherry, or port*
Dash cayenne pepper

In glass container with tight-fitting cover, blend all ingredients together. Cover tightly and store in refrigerator. Serve with crackers or breads. Makes 2 to 3 cups cheese spread.

CHEESE SAUCE

3 *tablespoons butter*
3 *tablespoons flour*
1½ *cups milk*
½ *to 1 cup grated or diced cheese*
½ *teaspoon salt*
½ *teaspoon dry mustard*

In small saucepan melt butter; stir in flour and seasonings. Stir in milk; heat, stirring constantly, until sauce is thickened. Reduce heat. Add cheese and stir until blended. Makes about 2 cups sauce.

BROILED CHEESE-BACON SANDWICH

2 *cups cheese, shredded*
2 *tablespoons ripe olives, chopped*
¼ *cup onion, minced*
1 *teaspoon parsley, chopped*
6 *slices bacon, cooked, drained, and chopped*
⅔ *cup mayonnaise*
¼ *teaspoon prepared mustard*
3 *or 4 sandwich buns, split*

In medium bowl blend cheese, olives, onions, parsley, and bacon. Add the mustard and mayonnaise; blend thoroughly. Mound mixture on each half of buns. Broil 5 inches from heat or bake at 400° until cheese is melted. Makes 6 or 8 open-face sandwiches.

CHEESE, CHEDDAR

How to Use: Use to make Welsh rarebit, cheese-beer soup.
Dice and mix with catsup, pickle relish, minced onion, and Worcestershire sauce. Use as appetizer dip or hot dog topping.
See "Cheese, General" section.

CHEESE, BLUE

How to Use: Crumble into tossed salads.

Stuff chunks of blue cheese into endive leaves; use as garnish for fruit salads or on cold plates.

Mix with ground beef, onion, salt, and Worcestershire. Broil burgers and serve on buns.

Sour cream sauce: Combine crumbled blue cheese with sour cream and Worcestershire; chill. Serve over hamburgers, salad greens, baked potatoes.

BLUE CHEESE SALAD DRESSING I

¼ *cup blue cheese, crumbled*
1 *cup buttermilk*

Combine blue cheese and buttermilk in blender or with electric beater. Chill. Serve over lettuce wedges.

BLUE CHEESE SALAD DRESSING II

1 *quart mayonnaise (not salad dressing)*
1 *cup buttermilk*
½ *cup blue cheese, crumbled*
⅓ *cup dried chives*
¼ *teaspoon white pepper*
¼ *teaspoon salt*
¼ *teaspoon Worcestershire sauce*

Combine mayonnaise, buttermilk, and blue cheese. Add remaining ingredients and mix well. Cover and chill several hours before using. Makes about 1 quart.

CHEESE, SWISS

How to Use: Use in fondues and quiches.

Use in Reuben and Poor Boy sandwiches.

Shred and serve over creamed eggs in Newburg sauce.

QUICHE LORRAINE

1 *9-inch pastry shell, unbaked*
1 *egg, beaten*

1 *cup evaporated milk*
½ *teaspoon salt*
½ *teaspoon Worcestershire sauce*
1 *cup Swiss cheese, shredded*
1 *(3½-ounce) can French-fried onions*
12 *slices bacon, fried and crumbled (or 1 cup cooked ham, minced)*

Combine egg, milk, salt, and Worcestershire. Stir in cheese. Sprinkle half the onions over crust. Pour egg-cheese mixture into crust. Sprinkle with remaining onions and the bacon or ham. Bake at 450° 15 minutes. Reduce heat to 350° and bake about 10 minutes longer or until filling is set. Cool 5 minutes before slicing. Serves 4 to 6 as a main dish.

COTTAGE CHEESE

How to Use: Use as a base for dips: Mix in blender with seafood or vegetable combinations; season to taste.

For a spicy dip, mix with canned chili with beans, season with hot pepper sauce and lemon juice. Chill before serving.

Herb cheese spread: Blend cottage cheese with equal amount of thick cream, salt, chives, parsley, and favorite herb; form into ball and chill.

Seafood appetizer ball: Mix equal amounts of cottage cheese and cooked shrimp or tuna with lemon juice, grated onion, prepared mustard, chutney, Worcestershire sauce, salt, and garlic powder; shape into ball and chill until firm.

Add a spoonful of cottage cheese to hot, spicy soups for a contrast in texture and temperature.

Season with such combinations as pineapple and carrot, minced parsley and shredded carrot, avocado and onion, or cucumber and onion; season to taste with Tabasco or Worcestershire sauce, or lemon juice or garlic salt. Serve on lettuce leaves or over sliced fruit.

Make a low-calorie salad dressing by blending cottage cheese with buttermilk (use about half as much buttermilk); add wine vinegar, parsley, and salt to taste.

Vegetable salad dressing: Combine equal amounts of cottage cheese and dairy sour cream; season to taste with chili sauce, lemon juice, and prepared horseradish; chill before using.

Add to molded gelatin salads along with fruit or vegetables; up to 1 cup cottage cheese may be added to a 3-ounce package of gelatin.

Mix with crushed pineapple and serve over an orange slice.

Top with mixture of crushed pineapple and small pieces of cooked prunes.

Use as base for sandwich fillings with such mixtures as grated carrot, sweet pickle relish, mayonnaise, crumbled bacon, salt, and pepper, or with minced onion, green pepper, salt, and paprika.

Add to scrambled eggs before cooking; up to ½ cup cottage cheese to each 4 eggs may be used. Season to taste.

Add to lasagna recipes.

Use in blintzes.

LAYERED CASSEROLE

½ *pound broad noodles, cooked and drained*
1 *teaspoon salt*
1 *pound ground beef*
¼ *teaspoon pepper*
2 *cups tomato sauce*
1 *teaspoon basil*
1 *cup cottage cheese*
½ *pound jack or cheddar cheese, grated, or 8 ounces cream cheese*
¼ *cup dairy sour cream*
⅓ *cup green onions, minced*
1 *tablespoon green pepper, minced*

If possible, prepare dish several hours before baking to let flavors blend. In medium skillet sauté the meat until no red color remains; drain excess fat. Add tomato sauce, salt, pepper, and basil; remove from heat. Combine cottage cheese, jack or cheddar or cream cheese, sour cream, onion, and green pepper. Layer noodle mixture and cheese mixture alternately in a greased 2-quart casserole. Pour meat sauce over all. Bake at 350° for 45 minutes or until heated through. Serves 4 to 6.

COTTAGE CHEESE PANCAKES

3 *eggs*
½ *cup cottage cheese*
⅓ *cup milk*

¼ cup flour
¼ teaspoon salt
⅛ teaspoon baking powder

In medium bowl beat eggs until light. In separate bowl mash cottage cheese until almost smooth; add to eggs and beat well. Blend in milk, flour, salt, and baking powder. Let batter stand 5 minutes. Drop batter by table-spoonfuls onto hot greased griddle. Bake until top is bubbly and edges lightly browned. Turn and bake other side. Serve at once with butter and jelly. Makes 12 small pancakes.

COTTAGE CHEESE BREAD PUDDING

2 cups milk
4 cups coarse bread crumbs
¼ cup butter, melted
⅔ cup sugar
2 eggs or 4 egg yolks
1 cup cottage cheese
¼ teaspoon salt
1 teaspoon vanilla
1 teaspoon cinnamon or nutmeg, if desired
½ cup raisins, if desired

In saucepan heat milk to scalding. Place bread crumbs in large bowl; pour milk over bread. In separate medium bowl, beat eggs; add sugar, salt, melted butter, vanilla, cottage cheese, and cinnamon or nutmeg and raisins, if desired. Pour mixture over bread and mix. Pour into greased 1½-quart baking dish. Bake at 350° for 40 to 45 minutes or until knife inserted into middle of pudding comes out clean. Serve warm. Serves 4 to 6.

CREAM

CREAM, LIGHT (coffee cream, half-and-half)

How to Use: Substitute for milk in many cooked recipes. Thin with water or milk if necessary.
Substitute in equal amounts for evaporated milk in recipes.
Pour over cereals, puddings, fresh fruits.
Use in making cream soups, à la King dishes, potato soup, Chicken Divan.

Use in place of condensed cream soups in many cooked recipes. It may be necessary to use additional thickening.

Use in powdered-sugar frostings.

CREAM, WHIPPING

How to Use: Frozen Whipped Cream Dollops: Whip cream until stiff. Add a little powdered sugar for sweetening. Drop in mounds of 2 tablespoons each on waxed paper or foil. Cover and freeze until firm; remove from paper and store in freezer container until needed. To use, remove from freezer and place on top of dessert.

Orange-Honey Syrup: Gently heat 10 minutes: 1 cup whipping cream, 1 cup honey, and ¼ cup butter. Add 2 tablespoons orange liqueur. Serve warm over ice cream, waffles or pancakes, poundcake, and so forth.

CREAM, SOURED

Any cream that sours despite present methods of pasteurization has spoiled and is better thrown away than eaten.

CREAM CHEESE

How to Use: Spread on pancakes. Top with maple syrup and chopped salted nuts.

Season as desired and use for appetizer dips. Possible combinations are cream cheese and blue cheese, cream cheese and sharp processed cheddar, cream cheese thinned with cream; seasonings include lemon juice, garlic salt, chili powder, curry, seasoned salt, herbs of choice. Other additions could include grated onion, nuts, chopped green or black olives, paprika, parsley.

Season to taste and use to stuff celery stalks or endive leaves. Seasonings may include onion juice, chives, lemon juice, parsley, stuffed olives, crisp bacon bits, or seasoned salt.

Use for sandwich spread. Possible combinations are with jam, marmalade, or jelly; seasoned as for stuffing celery stalks (above); mixed with chopped green olives topped with sliced chicken; mixed with chopped almonds, pecans, or walnuts; blended with blue cheese, butter, onion juice, Worcestershire, sherry, and salt; combined with shredded dried beef, horseradish, and thinned with milk or cream; mixed with other grated cheese; mixed with chopped ripe olives.

Cut in cubes and add to a variety of fruit or vegetable gelatin salads.

Topping for gelatin salads: Combine 6 ounces cream cheese at room temperature with ¼ cup light cream; mix until smooth. Spread over firmly jelled salad. Covers an 8-inch square surface.

Fruit topping: Beat together 3 ounces softened cream cheese with 2 tablespoons sugar, a dash salt, and 2 tablespoons evaporated milk or whole milk. Fold into 2 cups whipped topping. Spoon over fresh berries or other fruit.

Cream Frosting Glaze for Bars: Cream together 3 ounces cream cheese, 2 tablespoons butter, 1 cup powdered sugar, ½ teaspoon vanilla, dash of salt. Frosts a 9-by-13-inch or 11-by-15-inch pan.

Thick Frosting: Cream together 3 ounces softened cream cheese and ¼ cup butter. Stir in 1 tablespoon milk or cream and 1 teaspoon vanilla. Blend in 2 cups powdered sugar. Covers a 9-by-13-inch pan.

Fluffy Orange Frosting: Blend 3 ounces softened cream cheese, 3 tablespoons melted butter, 1 teaspoon grated orange rind, 2 tablespoons orange juice, and 1½ cups powdered sugar. Covers a 9-by-13-inch pan.

DAIRY SOUR CREAM

How to Use: Chip Dip: Blend ½ cup sour cream with ½ teaspoon dry salad dressing mix or with dry onion soup mix. Blend well. Chill before using.

Add sour cream to scrambled eggs (2 teaspoons per egg) just before eggs have completely set. If desired, add crumbled bacon also.

Add 1 to 3 teaspoons of sour cream to cottage cheese before serving.

Salad dressing: Blend sour cream with herbed salad dressing to taste. Add chopped green onions. Serve over salad greens or pour over hot cooked vegetables or on a cold vegetable platter.

Spoon a dollop of sour cream on top of hot soup for a cooling garnish.

Quick Sour Cream Sauce: Blend ½ cup sour cream with 1 can condensed cream soup; heat gently until warm. Serve over chicken, vegetables, meat loaf, croquettes, and so on.

Topping for cold beef sandwich: Combine ½ cup dairy sour cream, 2 teaspoons dry onion soup mix, freshly ground pepper and prepared horseradish to taste. Spread mixture on buttered bread; top with a slice of roast beef, lettuce, and a second slice of bread. Enough for 4 sandwiches.

Fish Sauce: ¼ cup sour cream, ¼ cup mayonnaise, dash of lemon juice and cayenne pepper. Or add drained pickle relish, onion salt, and curry powder.

Topping for fruit: Combine ½ cup sour cream and 2 tablespoons brown sugar. Chill, then serve over fresh or frozen fruit. Goes especially well with green grapes or blueberries.

SOUR CREAM–ORANGE SAUCE FRUIT TOPPING

2 *teaspoons butter*
⅓ *cup powdered sugar*
½ *teaspoon grated fresh orange rind*
2 *teaspoons orange juice*
½ *cup dairy sour cream*
1½ *cups blueberries, fresh or frozen*

In small bowl cream butter and sugar until smooth. Stir in orange rind and orange juice. Add sour cream and stir until smooth. Spoon over berries.

MILK

EVAPORATED MILK

How to Use: Substitute for light cream in many recipes.

Thin with equal parts water and use in place of whole milk.

Substitute for cream soups in a variety of cooked dishes.

Add to white sauces, cream soups.

Add up to ⅔ cup to 1 pound ground beef in making meat loaf or meat balls.

Use in sponges. (Whip cold evaporated milk. Serve into jelled fruit gelatin.)

Use in powdered sugar frostings in place of cream or milk.

MILK, SOURED

Present methods of pasteurization prevent milk from souring if properly stored. Pasteurized milk that has spoiled and soured should be thrown out.

SWEETENED CONDENSED MILK

How to Use: Hot Fudge Sauce: Mix sweetened condensed milk with an equal amount of chocolate sauce. Stir over low heat until mixture is bubbly. Serve warm.

Heavenly Hash: Melt 6 ounces semisweet chocolate pieces in large saucepan over medium heat. Stir until smooth. Remove from heat and slowly stir in ⅔ cup sweetened condensed milk. Add ½ pound miniature marshmallows and ½ cup pecan pieces. Drop by tablespoonfuls onto greased cookie sheet. Chill until firm.

MACAROONS

⅔ cup sweetened condensed milk
1 teaspoon vanilla
2⅔ cups flaked coconut
¾ teaspoon almond flavoring

In medium bowl, mix all ingredients well. Drop by teaspoonfuls 1 inch apart onto well-greased baking sheet. Bake at 350° 8 to 10 minutes or until lightly browned. Remove at once from baking sheet. Makes about 18 macaroons.

BERRY SHERBET

1½ cups fresh berries, such as strawberries or raspberries
⅓ cup powdered sugar
⅔ cup sweetened condensed milk
2 tablespoons lemon juice
2 egg whites

Force berries through a sieve. Add sugar and stir. In a large bowl combine sweetened condensed milk and lemon juice. Fold in mashed berries; chill. Beat egg whites until stiff but not dry; fold into chilled mixture. Place mixture in an ice cube tray and cover with aluminum foil. Freeze until a firm mush forms, about an hour. Turn into chilled medium bowl: break into pieces with a spoon, then beat until fluffy but not melted. Return to ice cube tray, cover, and freeze until firm. Serves 6.

CUSTARD SAUCE

⅔ cup sweetened condensed milk
1½ cups hot water
¼ teaspoon salt
2 eggs, slightly beaten
1 teaspoon vanilla

In top of double boiler combine sweetened condensed milk, water, and salt; blend well. Stir in eggs gradually. Cook over hot water for 20 minutes, stirring constantly, or until mixture coats a metal spoon. Remove from heat and place in top of double boiler over ice water. Add vanilla. Chill. Serve over fruit or cakes. Makes 2 cups sauce.

LEMON BUTTER CREAM FROSTING

¼ cup butter
1½ teaspoons grated lemon rind
⅔ cup sweetened condensed milk
3½ cups powdered sugar, sifted
1 to 2 tablespoons lemon juice

In medium bowl cream butter and lemon rind. Slowly stir in half of the sweetened condensed milk. Stir in sugar and remaining milk alternately, beating until smooth after each addition. Add lemon juice until desired flavor is obtained. Spread on cooled cake. Makes 2 cups frosting, enough to frost a 9-by-13-inch cake or two 8-inch cake layers.

CREAM FILLING WITH FRUIT

⅔ cup sweetened condensed milk
2 tablespoons lemon juice
½ cup fruit (fresh raspberries, strawberries, or peaches, sliced
    or mashed; or crushed pineapple)

In medium bowl combine sweetened condensed milk and lemon juice. Fold in fruit and stir until well blended. Spread over bottom layer of an 8- or 9-inch cake. Place top layer of cake over filling and frost as desired. Makes 1¼ cups filling, enough to fill two 8-inch cake layers.

Meat, Poultry, Fish, Eggs, and Beans

BACON, COOKED

How to Use: Add to scrambled eggs.

Add to hot vinegar dressings.

Add to bean, lentil, or potato soup.

Blend into egg salad sandwich spread.

Add to bacon, tomato, and lettuce sandwiches, or use as a topping for broiled cheese and tomato sandwiches.

Use in Welsh Rarebit.

Mix with cottage cheese, grated carrot, sweet pickle relish, mayonnaise, salt, and pepper for a sandwich filling.

Add to corn muffin batter before baking muffins.

Mix with peanut butter for a sandwich spread. Mix in applesauce if desired.

Sprinkle crumbled bacon and grated cheese over such cooked vegetables as cauliflower, Brussels sprouts, broccoli, corn, cabbage, and green pepper.

Sprinkle crumbled bacon over broiled tomatoes or baked potatoes.

Add crumbled bacon and chopped green onions to cooked peas. Moisten with dairy sour cream or mayonnaise and season to taste. Chill and serve on lettuce leaves.

Sprinkle crumbled bacon on soups as a garnish.

Sprinkle over baked squash.

Add to meat loaf mixture before baking.

BEEF, COOKED ROAST

How to Use: Cut in strips and add to chef salad.

Grind or mince to use in hash or sandwich fillings.

Slice and serve in hot gravy over bread or hot biscuits.

Add chunks to spaghetti sauce, soups, casseroles, macaroni and cheese.

Beef Dip: Combine ¼ cup chopped cooked beef with 1 cup dairy sour cream. Add salt, pepper, garlic salt, and hot pepper sauce to taste. Chill before serving.

Beef Burgundy: Heat strips of cooked beef and canned mushrooms in beef gravy. Add burgundy to taste. Serve over rice or noodles.

Freeze diced or sliced beef in gravy or broth. When you have the desired amount, heat in barbecue sauce or beef gravy for hot sandwiches.

QUICK BEEF STROGANOFF

3 *tablespoons flour*
1½ *teaspoons salt*
¼ *teaspoon pepper*
2 *cups cooked beef, sliced*
1 *clove garlic, minced*
¼ *cup vegetable oil*
½ *cup onion, chopped*
¼ *cup water*
1 *(10¾-ounce) can cream of chicken or mushroom soup*
4 *ounces canned mushrooms, drained*
1 *cup dairy sour cream*

Combine flour, salt, and pepper in paper bag or dish; coat beef with flour mixture. In large skillet heat oil; brown beef, then add onion and garlic. Sauté until onions are golden. Add water and stir. Add soup and mushrooms; heat gently until mixture is thick and meat is warmed through, about 5 minutes. Just before serving stir in sour cream; heat but do not boil. Serve over rice, noodles, or mashed potatoes. Serves 3 or 4.

BEEF-MACARONI BAKE

1 *medium onion, chopped*
2 *tablespoons vegetable oil*

2 cups cooked beef, diced
2 teaspoons garlic salt
¾ teaspoon basil
¼ teaspoon pepper
2 cups tomato sauce
1½ cups water
3 cups macaroni, uncooked
2 tablespoons Parmesan cheese, grated

In large skillet sauté onion in oil until soft. Stir in beef; brown lightly. Add garlic salt, basil, pepper, tomato sauce, and water; heat to boiling. Add macaroni and stir. Pour into 1½-quart greased baking dish. Cover and bake at 350° 1 hour or until macaroni is tender. Uncover, sprinkle with Parmesan cheese, and bake 10 minutes longer. Serves 4.

BEEF HASH CASSEROLE

1½ cups cooked beef, cubed
1 cup cooked potato, cubed
1 (5⅓-ounce) can evaporated milk
¼ cup parsley, minced
2 teaspoons Worcestershire sauce
1 teaspoon salt
⅛ teaspoon pepper
¼ cup onion, minced

In large bowl toss together all ingredients. Turn mixture into a lightly greased 1½-quart casserole. Bake uncovered at 350° for 30 minutes or until heated through. Serves 2 to 3.

BEEF STOVE-TOP SUPPER

2 cups cooked beef, cubed
3 cups raw potato, cubed
1 cup beef broth
1 (16-ounce) can stewed tomatoes
¾ teaspoon seasoned salt
  Dash pepper
1 cup onions, chopped

In medium saucepan combine all ingredients; bring to a boil. Cover and simmer until potatoes are tender, stirring occasionally. Serves 4.

BEEF AND TOMATOES IN GRAVY

1 (16-ounce) can tomatoes
1 (¾-ounce) envelope brown gravy mix or mushroom gravy
      mix (or 1 cup beef gravy)
1 tablespoon wine vinegar or ⅓ cup dry white wine
2 to 3 cups cooked beef, cubed
⅓ cup sliced ripe olives, if desired
2 teaspoons parsley, chopped

In medium skillet combine gravy mix or gravy, tomatoes and wine or vinegar; bring to a boil. Reduce heat, cover, and simmer 5 minutes. Add beef and simmer 10 minutes. Thicken with small amount of cornstarch mixed with a little water, if desired. Serve garnished with olives and parsley. Serves 4.

ORIENTAL BEEF SKILLET

1½ to 2 cups cooked beef, cut in strips
2 tablespoons vegetable oil
1 medium onion, chopped
1 (10-ounce) package frozen French-style green beans
¾ cup liquid (mushroom liquid plus water)
1 cup celery, sliced on diagonal
1 tablespoon cornstarch
2 tablespoons soy sauce
1 (4-ounce) can mushrooms (reserve liquid)
⅓ cup water chestnuts, drained, if desired

In medium skillet brown beef in oil. Add onions and celery; sauté until tender. Add beans and ¾ cup liquid from mushrooms. Cover and cook until beans are tender. Combine cornstarch and soy sauce with a small amount of water. Add to skillet, cooking and stirring until shiny. Add mushrooms and water chestnuts, if desired. Serve over hot rice. Serves 4.

BARBECUE BEEF SANDWICHES

1 medium onion, sliced
2 tablespoons vegetable oil
2 to 3 cups cooked beef, thinly sliced
1 cup catsup
2 tablespoons prepared mustard
2 tablespoons brown sugar
1 teaspoon vinegar
½ teaspoon ground cloves
8 sandwich buns

In medium saucepan sauté onion in oil until soft. Add beef, catsup, mustard, brown sugar, vinegar, and cloves. Add a small amount of water, if desired. Simmer uncovered on very low heat until mixture is thick. Add salt and pepper to taste. Serve on buns. Makes 8 sandwiches.

BEEF-POTATO SALAD

2 cups cooked beef, sliced
1½ to 2 cups cooked potatoes, sliced
½ green pepper, minced
¼ cup celery, diced
½ cup dill pickles, sliced
1 small onion, cut in rings

Dressing:
⅔ cups vegetable oil
⅓ cup white wine vinegar
½ teaspoon salt
1 clove garlic, crushed
Pepper to taste

Combine dressing ingredients in jar: cover and shake. In a large bowl with cover, combine beef, potatoes, green pepper, celery, pickles, and onions. Pour dressing over salad and toss. Cover and chill several hours. Serves 4 or 5.

HEARTY BEEF SALAD

2 cups cooked beef, cubed
1 cup kidney beans, drained
¾ cup celery, diced
¼ cup onion, minced
2 hard-cooked eggs, chopped

Dressing:
½ cup salad dressing or mayonnaise
1 tablespoon pickle relish
1 tablespoon chili sauce
¼ teaspoon salt
Lettuce

Combine salad ingredients in medium bowl. Combine dressing ingredients; pour over salad mixture and toss lightly. Cover and chill several hours. Serve in lettuce cups. Serves 4.

CORNED BEEF, COOKED

How to Use: Mince and add to scrambled eggs.

Make a sandwich or cracker spread by mixing minced corned beef with mayonnaise and pickle relish.

Slice and use for Reuben sandwiches: Layer sliced corned beef, sliced mild cheese, drained sauerkraut, and Thousand Island or Russian dressing on pumpernickel or rye bread. Grill if desired.

Add to macaroni and cheese.

Add to scalloped potatoes. Add sliced cabbage, if desired, and add a small amount of Dijon mustard to the cream sauce.

CORNED BEEF AND NOODLE BAKE

1½ cups noodles, cooked
1 (10¾-ounce) can cream of chicken soup
1 cup mild cheese, shredded
1 cup milk
1½ cups corned beef, diced
½ cup onion, chopped
Bread crumbs

Blend soup, cheese, and milk. Add remaining ingredients except for crumbs. Place in buttered 1½-quart baking dish. Top with crumbs. Bake at 350° 45 minutes. Serves 2 to 4.

CORNED BEEF HASH AS-YOU-LIKE-IT

Corned beef, chopped
Cooked potatoes, diced
Salt and pepper to taste
Minced onion to taste
Chopped parsley, if desired

Optional seasonings:
A pinch of nutmeg
Green pepper, minced
Pimiento, chopped
Chopped cooked beets

In medium bowl combine equal amounts of corned beef and potatoes; season to taste with salt, pepper, minced onion, and other seasonings as desired.

Moisten with milk or potato-cooking liquid. Turn into greased hot skillet or baking dish. Cook on stove top over low heat until browned, then fold over like an omelet. Or bake at 350° for 20 to 30 minutes. If desired, top with poached eggs or creamed peas. Or stuff hash in parboiled hollowed-out onions, top with bread crumbs and Parmesan cheese, and bake. Or use in baked stuffed tomatoes.

BEEF LIVER

How to Use: Use in liver pâté.

Cut into small slices, dip in wheat germ, and sauté in vegetable oil until tender, about 5 minutes. Season to taste.

Brown floured liver in vegetable oil, then simmer with onions, celery, green pepper, and canned tomatoes or tomato sauce until tender. Season to taste. Serve over rice.

Grind cooked leftover liver, combine with mayonnaise and seasonings, and serve on crackers or celery sticks.

LIVER WITH GREEN ONIONS

1 *pound beef liver, sliced*
2 *tablespoons flour*
1 *tablespoon brown sugar*
1 *tablespoon dry mustard*
2 *tablespoons vegetable oil*
  Salt and pepper
12 *green onions*
¼ *cup water or white wine*

Combine flour, sugar, and mustard; dredge liver in flour mixture. In large heavy skillet brown liver in oil. Cut white portion of onions into 4-inch lengths; chop green tops into ¼-inch sections. Add onions and tops to liver. Pour on water or wine. Cover and simmer until liver is tender, about 8 minutes. Serve at once. Serves 4.

HAM

How to Use: Fry slices for breakfast meat.

Slice and use for sandwiches.

Grind with sweet pickle relish for sandwich or cracker spread. Moisten with salad dressing, if necessary.

Mince and make a sandwich filling with chopped celery and onions, salt and pepper to taste. Moisten with mayonnaise.

Add to the following soups: pea, bean, lentil, potato, minestrone.

Chop and add to baked beans.

Pie-Chams: Brown slices of ham and pineapple slices in butter. Place on toasted sandwich bun or English muffin halves. Top with slice of cheddar cheese. Broil until cheese melts.

Quick Scalloped Ham and Potatoes: Layer slices of ham with raw onion and raw potato slices, salt, and pepper; over each layer pour cream soup thinned with a little milk. Cover and bake at 375° 1 hour.

Ham stuffing for squash: Mix minced ham with small amounts of onion, celery, and green pepper that have been sautéed in butter. Add fresh bread crumbs, a little salt, and freshly baked acorn squash scooped from its shell. Stir all ingredients and pile into squash shells. Sprinkle with buttered bread crumbs. Bake 10 minutes until heated through.

BAKED HAM AND EGG SANDWICHES

1 *cup cooked ham, chopped*
½ *cup cheese, diced*
2 *tablespoons onion, chopped*
2 *hard-cooked eggs, chopped*
2 *tablespoons green olives, chopped*
4 *tablespoons mayonnaise*
3 *tablespoons chili sauce or catsup*
8 *sandwich buns, buttered*

Combine all ingredients except buns. Spread mixture on buns; wrap tightly in foil. Heat at 400° 15 to 18 minutes. Makes 8 sandwiches.

BARBECUED HAM SANDWICHES

½ *cup catsup*
2 *tablespoons vegetable oil*
1 *tablespoon vinegar*
2 *tablespoons water*
3 *tablespoons brown sugar*
1 *cup pineapple tidbits*
½ *cup green pepper, chopped*

1 *cup ham, sliced in small pieces*
Sandwich buns, warmed and buttered

In small saucepan combine catsup, oil, vinegar, water, and brown sugar. Simmer uncovered for 15 minutes. Add pineapple, green pepper, and ham. Simmer 10 minutes or longer. Serve in buns. Serves 2 or 3.

DENVER HAM SANDWICHES

6 *sandwich buns or English muffins, sliced, toasted, and*
buttered
6 *slices cooked ham*
4 *eggs*
¼ *cup milk*
¼ *teaspoon salt*
Dash pepper
2 *tablespoons vegetable oil*
¼ *cup green onions, chopped*
6 *tomato slices*
6 *slices cheddar cheese*

Place ham slice on lower half of buns. Beat together eggs, milk, salt, and pepper. In medium skillet, heat oil and cook onions until tender. Add egg mixture and cook, stirring frequently, until eggs are set. Place a spoonful of eggs on top of ham slice; cover with tomato slice and cheese slice. Place on cookie sheet and broil until cheese melts. Top with other half of bun. Makes 6 sandwiches.

CAULIFLOWER-HAM AU GRATIN

4 *cups cauliflower*
2 *cups ham, cubed*
½ *cup canned mushrooms*
4 *tablespoons butter or margarine*
⅓ *cup flour*
1 *cup milk*
1 *cup cheddar cheese, cubed*
½ *cup dairy sour cream*
1 *cup soft bread crumbs*
1 *tablespoon butter or margarine, melted*

Break cauliflower into buds; cook, covered, in salted water until barely tender; drain. In medium saucepan, melt 4 tablespoons butter; stir in flour. Add milk; cook and stir until mixture thickens. Add cheese and sour cream; stir until cheese melts. Add cauliflower, ham, and mushrooms. Place in greased 2-quart baking dish. Combine bread crumbs and 1 tablespoon melted butter; sprinkle over top. Bake, uncovered, at 325° 40 minutes. Serves 4 to 6.

EASY HAM AND RICE CASSEROLE

1 (10¾-ounce) can condensed cream of mushroom soup
1½ to 2 cups cooked ham, cubed
1⅓ cups cooked rice
2 cups green beans, cooked and drained
2 tablespoons onions, chopped
Fine dry bread crumbs

Combine all ingredients except crumbs in a greased 1½-quart baking dish. Sprinkle with crumbs. Bake at 350° for 30 to 40 minutes. Serves 3 or 4.

HAM AND HASH BROWNS

3 cups frozen hash brown potatoes
2 tablespoons onions, chopped
1½ to 2 cups cooked ham, cubed
⅓ cup vegetable oil
2 tablespoons green pepper, chopped
½ teaspoon salt
Pepper to taste

Mix all ingredients in bowl. Heat oil in large skillet to medium high heat or 375°. Carefully pour in potato-ham mixture. Cover and cook for 8 to 10 minutes. Stir once during cooking. Serves 2 to 4.

JAMBALAYA

2 tablespoons vegetable oil
3 onions, thinly sliced
1 clove garlic, minced
1 green pepper, diced
1 cup vegetable or chicken broth
2 cups canned or fresh tomatoes, chopped
1 cup rice, uncooked
¼ teaspoon thyme
¼ teaspoon chili powder
1 tablespoon parsley, chopped
1 teaspoon salt
¼ teaspoon pepper
2 cups ham, diced

In medium saucepan sauté onion, garlic, and green pepper in oil. Add broth and tomatoes; bring to boil. Slowly stir in rice. Add thyme, chili powder, parsley, salt, and pepper. Cover and simmer 15 to 20 minutes or until rice is tender. Add ham; heat until meat is warmed through. Serves 6.

LAMB, COOKED ROAST

How to Use: Grind and use to stuff green peppers, onions, tomatoes, or zucchini.

Grind and use in Moussaka.

Add to Scotch broth (barley soup).

Lamb-Cheese Casserole: Arrange diced cooked lamb, tomato sauce, and sliced mild cheese in shallow baking pan. Sprinkle with oregano and paprika. Bake at 350° 30 minutes.

Lamb-Pea Casserole: In ovenproof skillet sauté ½ cup chopped onion, 1 stalk chopped celery, and ½ cup fresh or frozen peas. Cook 5 minutes. Add 1 to 2 cups diced cooked lamb, 1 teaspoon Worcestershire; simmer 10 minutes. Add 2 cups gravy or white sauce, salt and pepper to taste. Sprinkle with parsley, crumbs, and diced cheese. Place under broiler until cheese melts.

Lamb Supper Salad: Combine chopped cooked lamb, cooked peas, diced celery, and chopped toasted walnuts; moisten with mayonnaise seasoned with mustard, tarragon, or mint. Add salt and pepper to taste. Serve on lettuce.

CURRIED LAMB

1½ *cups cooked lamb, diced*
¼ *cup onion, sliced*
2 *teaspoons curry powder*
2 *tablespoons butter, margarine, or vegetable oil*
1 *(10¾-ounce) can cream soup or 1¼ cups medium white sauce*
1 *(10-ounce) package frozen peas or 1½ cups cooked peas*
2 *to 3 cups cooked rice*

Meat, Poultry, Fish, Eggs, and Beans **37**

In medium skillet sauté lamb, onion, and curry powder in butter until onion is tender. Add cream soup and peas; thin mixture with milk or water to desired consistency. Simmer 10 minutes. Serve over rice. Serves 4.

SHEPHERD'S PIE

> 2 *tablespoons vegetable oil*
> 2 *cups diced cooked lamb (or 1 pound ground lamb)*
> ¼ *cup onion, chopped*
> 1 *cup cooked peas*
> 1 *cup celery, diced*
> 1 *cup cooked sliced carrots, if desired*
> 2 *cups gravy*
> ⅛ *teaspoon marjoram*
> 1 *teaspoon salt*
> ⅛ *teaspoon pepper*
> 2 *cups mashed potatoes*

In ovenproof skillet cook onion and celery in oil until onion is golden. Add lamb and cook until meat is lightly browned. Drain off excess fat. Stir in gravy, peas, carrots, and seasonings. Place spoonfuls of potatoes around edge of skillet. Bake at 350° 30 minutes or until potatoes are browned. Serve at once. Serves 4.

MEAT LOAF

How to Use: Slice thin, sauté briefly, and serve on bread for an open-face or closed sandwich.

Add to minestrone, bean soups.

Crumble and use in stuffing mixtures for stuffed green peppers, tomatoes, and zucchini.

Cut in cubes and add to homemade pizza.

Quick pizza sandwich: Spread spaghetti sauce on English muffins. Add meat loaf and grated mild cheese. Broil until cheese melts.

MISCELLANEOUS MEAT

How to Use: Freeze leftover meat until enough accumulates to make desired recipe.

Sandwich filling: Combine 1 cup ground or minced cooked meat, 1 tablespoon minced onion, 2 tablespoons pickle relish, salt and pepper to taste, and mayonnaise. Chill until ready to use.

Combine with rice or crumbs to stuff onions, green peppers, tomatoes, or cabbage. Serve with tomato sauce.

Broiled Cheese-Meat Muffins: Spread halved English muffins with butter and either mustard, catsup, or mayonnaise. Add slices of cooked meat; season as desired with salt, pepper, and spices. Broil until warm. Top each sandwich with cheese; broil until cheese melts.

Add to soups, such as vegetable, split pea, lentil, or minestrone.

Add to rice or macaroni salads.

Add to stews.

Grind and use for hash.

Add to tamales, enchiladas, Spanish rice, chili, or Jambalaya.

Use in egg rolls and fried rice.

Add to spaghetti sauce, lasagna, and pizza.

Use in soufflés and crêpes.

Brown and add to baked beans, macaroni and cheese, scrambled eggs, and casseroles.

Add to Paella or Moussaka.

Chop meat and add to white sauce, undiluted canned cream soups, or seasoned brown gravy; serve over rice, noodles, biscuits, potatoes, croquettes, toast, toast cups, or baked acorn squash halves.

Stir-Fried Meat: Slice meat thinly; fry in a small amount of oil over high heat in large pan along with slivers of garlic, onion, and desired vegetables. Add a dash of soy sauce and ginger. Serve over rice.

Grind meat for meat loaf. Mix with 1 egg for each 2 cups of meat. Add bread crumbs, milk, chopped leftover vegetables if desired, grated cheese if desired, and herbs and seasonings to taste. Bake 1 hour at 350°.

Make homemade frozen dinners from leftover meats. Add potatoes, gravy, vegetables—whatever cooked foods are left over from dinner. Cover tightly with foil and freeze.

MEAT CREOLE

1 *large onion, chopped*
¼ *cup green pepper, chopped*
¼ *cup celery, chopped*
1 *tablespoon vegetable oil*
1 *teaspoon salt*
1 *teaspoon chili powder*
1 *teaspoon sugar*
⅛ *teaspoon pepper*
¼ *teaspoon basil, oregano, or savory*
2 *cups cooked meat, diced*
1 *(8-ounce) can tomato sauce*
1 *to 2 cups gravy (or beef broth thickened with flour)*
Cooked rice or noodles, if desired

In medium skillet sauté onion, green pepper, and celery in oil until tender but not brown. Add remaining ingredients except rice. Simmer 10 minutes. Serve over cooked rice or noodles. Serves 3 or 4.

GOULASH

2 *tablespoons vegetable oil*
2 *large onions, coarsely chopped*
2 *cups cooked meat, diced*
1 *tablespoon paprika*
Salt to taste
1 *(6-ounce) can (or less) tomato paste*
1 *cup beef broth*
1 *medium clove minced garlic, if desired*
¼ *to 1 cup cooked vegetables, if desired*
Raw celery or green pepper
Cooked rice or noodles, if desired

In medium skillet, sauté onions, raw vegetables, and minced garlic in oil until browned. Add paprika, tomato paste, meat, and beef broth; heat thoroughly. Add cooked vegetables, if desired, and heat until warm. Add salt to taste. A small amount of white wine or dairy sour cream may be added just before serving. Serve over rice or noodles, if desired. Serves 4.

CHOW MEIN

2 tablespoons vegetable oil
1 to 2 cups onions, sliced
1½ cups celery, sliced on diagonal
1½ to 2 cups cooked meat, cubed or cut in small slices
2 cups broth or water
1 tablespoon molasses
¼ cup cornstarch
Salt to taste
2 teaspoons sugar
Water chestnuts, bean sprouts, or canned mushrooms, if
desired
Chow mein noodles

In medium skillet heat oil. Add meat and stir-fry quickly. Add onions and celery; stir-fry until vegetables are barely tender. Add broth. Cover and simmer until vegetables are tender. Push meat-vegetable mixture to outer rim of pan, making a well in the center. Combine molasses and cornstarch with a small amount of water; pour mixture into well, then mix thoroughly with the meat-vegetable mixture. Add salt and sugar; stir thoroughly. Add water chestnuts, bean sprouts, or canned mushrooms. Serve at once over noodles. Serves 4 to 6.

RISOTTO

2 cups cooked meat, cubed
2 tablespoons vegetable oil
Garlic salt to taste
Salt and pepper to taste
⅓ cup onion, diced
⅓ cup green pepper, chopped
1 clove garlic, minced
⅓ cup celery, chopped
½ cup uncooked rice
1 (4-ounce) can mushrooms, undrained
1 (16-ounce) can tomatoes

In large skillet brown meat in oil. Sprinkle with garlic salt, salt, and pepper. Set aside. Sauté onion, green pepper, garlic, and celery until golden. Add rice and stir until coated with pan drippings. Add more oil if needed. Stir in meat. Pour mushrooms and tomatoes on top of meat-vegetable-rice mixture. Cover tightly; cook slowly until rice is tender and liquid is absorbed. Serves 4 to 6.

COLONIAL GOULASH

3 tablespoons butter or margarine
2 medium onions, sliced
1 cup celery, sliced
2½ cups cooked meat, cubed or sliced
1½ teaspoons salt
⅛ teaspoon pepper
⅓ cup Parmesan cheese, grated
1½ cups evaporated milk (or 1 can cream soup plus ½ cup milk)
2 tablespoons parsley, chopped
2 cups noodles, cooked

In medium skillet sauté onion and celery in butter. Add meat and heat gently until warmed. Combine salt, pepper, Parmesan cheese, and evaporated milk; add to meat mixture and heat until warmed through. Serve over noodles. Garnish with parsley. Serves 6.

FIVE-LAYER DINNER

2 or 3 strips bacon, partially cooked and drained
1 to 2 cups cooked meat, cubed
1½ cups raw carrots, sliced
1 medium onion, sliced
2 or 3 medium raw potatoes, sliced
   Salt and pepper to taste
1 cup water

Place all ingredients except water by layers in greased 2-quart casserole. Salt and pepper all layers except bacon. Add the water; cover and bake at 350° about 1 hour. Serves 3 or 4.

QUICK AND EASY OVEN DINNER

1 (10¾-ounce) can cream soup
1 cup noodles, uncooked
1 (10-ounce) package frozen vegetables such as beans, peas,
   or mixed vegetables
1½ to 2 cups cooked meat, cubed
   Crumb or cheese topping, if desired

Into greased 2-quart casserole pour ½ can of soup. Add noodles and frozen vegetables. Add meat and pour over remaining soup. Cover and bake at 350° 1 hour. Add crumbs or grated cheese, if desired, and bake uncovered 10 minutes. Serves 4.

USE-IT-UP-CROQUETTES

2 cups cooked meat, minced
½ to 1 cup thick white sauce or gravy, cooled
1 egg
2 tablespoons onion, grated
Salt and pepper to taste
1 tablespoon parsley
Optional seasonings: basil, paprika, dill weed,
Worcestershire, or chili sauce
Up to 1 cup cooked vegetables, if desired
¾ cup dry bread crumbs, wheat germ, or cracker crumbs
Topping: 1½ cups white sauce, cheese sauce, or tomato
sauce

In medium bowl, combine meat, white sauce or gravy, egg, onion, parsley, seasonings, and cooked vegetables. Form into round or oblong patties; roll in crumbs or sprinkle with crumbs. Mixture may seem runny but will solidify when cooked. Gently place patties in baking dish. Bake at 350° 20 minutes. Top with white sauce, cheese sauce, or tomato sauce. Serves 3 or 4.

TASTY BROILED SANDWICHES

4 slices bread
2 cups cheddar cheese, shredded
⅓ cup mayonnaise
2 tablespoons barbecue sauce
1 teaspoon onion, minced
Softened butter
½ to 1 cup cooked meat, diced

Combine cheese, mayonnaise, barbecue sauce, meat, and onion. Toast bread on one side under broiler. Spread untoasted side with butter, then with cheese-meat mixture. Broil until cheese melts. Serves 4.

COLD MARINATED MEAT

2 cups cooked roast beef, pork, veal or lamb, cut in narrow
strips
1 cup onion, chopped
2 tablespoons parsley, chopped
⅛ teaspoon tarragon or savory
Pepper to taste
¼ cup cider or wine vinegar
¼ cup vegetable oil
½ teaspoon dry mustard
Dash Tabasco

Combine all ingredients in shallow dish. Cover and marinate several hours in refrigerator. Serve chilled. Serves 4.

PORK, COOKED ROAST

How to Use: Add to baked beans, to pea, bean, or lentil soup.
Use in chow mein and chop suey.
Cube and add to scalloped potatoes.
Add chunks to cooked noodles; top with cheese sauce and bread crumbs. Bake at 350° 35 to 40 minutes.
Utilize all meat from a pork roast by simmering the bones in seasoned water or broth for 2 hours or until meat falls easily from the bones. Debone meat and use in any of the following recipes.

SWEET-SOUR PORK

1½ to 2 cups lean cooked pork, cubed
⅓ cup green pepper, diced
½ clove garlic, minced
2 tablespoons butter or vegetable oil
¼ cup cider vinegar
1 cup chicken broth
⅓ cup pineapple juice
½ teaspoon salt
2 tablespoons soy sauce
4 tablespoons cornstarch
⅓ cup sugar
⅔ cup pineapple tidbits, drained (reserve juice to use above)
Hot cooked rice

This dish is best when prepared a few hours before serving. In medium saucepan, sauté pork, green pepper, and garlic in butter; set aside. Heat vinegar, ¾ cup chicken broth, pineapple juice, soy sauce, sugar, and salt to boiling. In small bowl mix cornstarch and ¼ cup chicken broth. Add to mixture in saucepan and cook, stirring constantly, until mixture thickens. Add pork, vegetables, and pineapple. Heat thoroughly. Refrigerate until serving time. Heat and serve over hot cooked rice. Serves 4 to 6.

QUICK PORK CURRY

¼ cup onion, chopped
1 canned or raw tomato, peeled and chopped
1 to 2 teaspoons curry powder

¼ teaspoon salt
1 tablespoon vegetable oil
1 (10¾-ounce) can cream soup
½ cup milk
1½ to 2 cups cooked pork, cubed
1 cup dairy sour cream
Hot cooked rice
Sliced green onion for garnish

In medium skillet sauté onion, tomato, curry powder, and salt in oil until tender. Stir in soup and milk; blend until smooth. Add pork and simmer 10 minutes. Stir in sour cream; heat but do not boil. Serve over hot rice. Sprinkle with sliced green onions. Serves 3 or 4.

PORK-YAM HASH

¼ cup onion, chopped
4 tablespoons butter or margarine
2 cups cooked pork, chopped
2 cups cooked yams, mashed
⅓ cup evaporated milk or cream
½ teaspoon cinnamon
¼ teaspoon salt
1 cup crushed pineapple, drained
2 tablespoons brown sugar
½ cup chopped nuts, if desired

In medium skillet sauté onion in butter until soft. Stir in pork; cook until slightly browned. Add yams, milk, cinnamon, and salt: simmer, uncovered for 10 minutes. Spread pineapple over pork mixture. Sprinkle brown sugar over pineapple. Top with nuts, if desired. Cover and heat gently 3 to 5 minutes or until sugar melts. Serves 4.

SHORT-CUT CASSOULET

2 tablespoons vegetable oil or bacon drippings
1 cup celery, sliced
½ cup onion, chopped
½ cup green pepper, chopped
1 clove garlic, minced
1 to 2 cups cooked pork, diced
1 (16-ounce) can pork and beans
1 (16-ounce) can lima beans, undrained
1 (6-ounce) can tomato paste
1 teaspoon salt
Up to 2 cups additional chopped meat, if desired

Meat, Poultry, Fish, Eggs, and Beans **45**

In medium skillet sauté celery, onion, green pepper, and garlic in vegetable oil or bacon drippings. Stir in remaining ingredients. Simmer uncovered 15 minutes or longer. Flavor improves with long, gentle heating. Or let stand in refrigerator and reheat before serving. Serves 5 or 6.

ORIENTAL PORK SALAD

> 3 cups cabbage (green or Chinese), thinly sliced
> ¾ cup cooked rice
> ⅔ cup peas, cooked
> 1 to 2 cups cooked pork, diced
> ⅓ cup water chestnuts, drained and sliced
> 2 tablespoons green onions, sliced
> ¼ cup mayonnaise
> ¼ cup dairy sour cream
> ½ teaspoon celery salt
> ¼ teaspoon salt
> Pepper to taste

In large bowl toss together cabbage, rice, peas, pork, water chestnuts, and onions. Combine mayonnaise, sour cream, celery salt, and salt; add to salad and toss. Chill before serving. Serves 2 to 4.

BARBECUED PORK SANDWICH

> ⅓ cup onion, chopped
> 2 tablespoons vegetable oil
> 1 (8-ounce) can tomato sauce
> 4 tablespoons brown sugar
> 2 teaspoons Worcestershire sauce
> 2 teaspoons lemon juice
> 2 teaspoons prepared mustard
> 2 cups cooked pork, cubed
> 4 sandwich buns, split and warmed

In medium skillet sauté onion in oil until tender. Add tomato sauce, brown sugar, Worcestershire, lemon juice, and mustard; simmer, uncovered, about 20 minutes. Add pork: heat 10 minutes. Spoon over buns. Serves 4.

CHICKEN, COOKED

How to Use: Serve on bread as hot or cold sandwich.
Mince for sandwich spread.

Slice and serve cold with salads or vegetables, as desired.

Make chicken salad to serve on sandwiches, in stuffed tomatoes, or to heat foil-covered in oven on hamburger buns.

Use interchangeably with turkey in most recipes.

Use in Chicken Divan, Chicken à la King, Curried Chicken.

Quick Creamed Chicken: Heat 2 cups chopped cooked chicken, 1 cup cooked peas, 2 teaspoons minced onion, 2 tablespoons chopped pimiento, 1/2 teaspoon salt, 1/8 teaspoon pepper, 1 can condensed cream of chicken soup, and 1 teaspoon lemon juice. Simmer 10 minutes. Serve over toast or rice.

BASIC CHICKEN SALAD

2 *cups cooked chicken, cubed*
1 *cup celery, chopped*
1 *tablespoon lemon juice*
½ *cup mayonnaise*
3 *hard-cooked eggs, chopped*
  Salt and pepper to taste

In medium bowl combine chicken, celery, lemon juice, salt, and pepper. Add mayonnaise and blend well. Fold in eggs. Chill before serving. Use as sandwich filling or mound on lettuce leaves or in tomato cups for salad. Garnish as desired. Serves 6.

ORIENTAL CHICKEN SALAD

2 *cups cooked chicken, cut in chunks*
1 *cup celery, chopped*
⅔ *to 1 cup water chestnuts, drained and sliced*
1 *tablespoon pimientos, drained and chopped*
½ *cup bamboo shoots, drained and sliced*
2 *green onions, slice thin*
¾ *to 1 cup mayonnaise*
2 *tablespoons soy sauce*
1 *tablespoon lemon juice*
  Salad greens

In medium bowl combine chicken and vegetables. In separate bowl combine mayonnaise, soy sauce, and lemon juice. Chill both mixtures separately for several hours. At serving time toss dressing and chicken mixture. Serve on greens. Serves 4 to 6.

HAWAIIAN CHICKEN

2 *tablespoons butter or margarine*
2 *green onions with tops, chopped*
1 *small clove garlic, minced*
1 *tablespoon flour*
½ *teaspoon salt*
½ *cup chicken broth*
1½ *cups chicken, cooked and diced*
    Up to 1 cup of any combination of: water chestnuts, bamboo
      shoots, mushroom slices
1¼ *cups pineapple tidbits, drained*
2 *tablespoons pimientos, chopped*
    Chow mein noodles or rice

In large skillet melt butter; add onion and garlic and cook until tender. Blend in flour and salt. Add broth. Cook until mixture comes to a boil. Add chicken; heat until thoroughly warm. Add remaining ingredients except noodles and heat only until warmed through. Serve over noodles or rice. Serves 2 or 3.

CHICKEN-BROCCOLI CASSEROLE

2½ *cups broccoli, cooked until barely tender*
2 *cups cooked chicken, sliced*
½ *cup mayonnaise*
¼ *cup milk*
1 *(10¾-ounce) can cream of chicken soup*

Place broccoli in 11-by-7-inch baking dish. Cover with chicken slices. Combine soup, mayonnaise, and milk; pour over chicken. Bake, uncovered, at 325° 30 minutes. Serves 4.

CHICKEN GIBLETS (Includes Gizzards and Hearts)

How to Use: Freeze uncooked giblets until you have enough to fix in desired recipes.

Cook giblets until tender in salted water, seasoned with celery leaves and sliced onions. Cool and dice, removing connecting tissue. Add to chopped cooked chicken in casseroles, salads, and creamed dishes.

Add cooked chopped giblets to corn chowder.

Use chopped giblets in cream or brown gravy or in stuffings.

CHICKEN GIBLETS IN GRAVY

> 1 *pound gizzards and hearts, cooked and sliced*
> ¼ *cup onion, chopped*
> 1 *cup celery, diced*
> 2 *tablespoons vegetable oil*
> 1¼ *cups gravy, or 1 (10½-ounce) can beef gravy*
> ¼ *cup canned mushrooms, if desired*
> ¼ *cup dry white wine*
> ½ *teaspoon salt*
> ½ *teaspoon dried tarragon*
>   *Dash pepper*
> 1 *tablespoon cornstarch*
> 1 *tablespoon cold water*
>   *Cooked rice, toast or noodles*

In medium skillet sauté onion and celery in oil until tender. Add giblets, gravy, mushrooms, wine, salt, tarragon, and pepper. Cover and simmer 5 minutes. Combine cornstarch and water; stir into gravy-meat mixture. Cook and stir until bubbly. Serve over rice, toast, or noodles. Serves 3 or 4.

CHICKEN GIBLETS PAPRIKASH

> 1 *pound gizzards and hearts, cooked and sliced*
> 1 *cup onions, chopped*
> 3 *tablespoons butter or margarine*
> 1 *tablespoon paprika*
> 1 *tomato, peeled, seeded, and chopped*
> 1 *cup broth*
> ½ *cup dairy sour cream*
> 2 *tablespoons flour*
>   *Salt and pepper to taste*
>   *Hot cooked rice or noodles*

In medium saucepan sauté onions in butter until golden. Add paprika and gizzards; cook 3 minutes. Add tomato and broth; cover and simmer 30 minutes. In small bowl combine dairy sour cream and flour; add to meat-vegetable mixture, and cook until smooth and thickened. Season to taste. Serve over noodles or rice. Serves 3 or 4.

CHICKEN LIVER

How to Use: Make into pâté.

Add to recipes for chicken giblets in gravy or white sauce.

Coat with seasoned flour and sauté in butter along with sliced onions. Add to white sauce or cream soup. Add sautéed green pepper and pimiento strips. If desired add a little dry sherry. Serve over patty shells or rice.

Sauté sliced mushrooms and onions in butter until onions are golden. Add sliced liver and sauté 3 minutes. Add salt and pepper to taste. Add dry white wine and cook 2 minutes. Serve over toast.

CRISP CHICKEN LIVERS

1 pound chicken livers, cut in halves
1 cup Saltine cracker crumbs
1 teaspoon garlic salt
1 teaspoon onion salt
¼ cup butter or margarine, melted

Combine cracker crumbs, melted butter, garlic salt, and onion salt. Roll livers in mixture. Place on flat baking sheet. Bake at 350° 20 to 30 minutes or until liver is tender and browned. Turn livers after 15 minutes of baking. Serve hot with mustard sauce. Serves 4 to 6 as an appetizer.

Mustard Sauce: Combine and chill: ½ cup prepared tartar sauce, 2 tablespoons prepared mustard, ¼ cup milk, and 2 tablespoons minced chives.

TURKEY, COOKED ROAST

How to Use: Substitute for chicken in many recipes.

Chop and add to vegetable soup, or bean or minestrone soup.

Use in Turkey Divan.

Heat in white sauce using chicken or turkey broth as liquid with mushrooms, onion, green pepper, parsley, seasonings to taste. Add sherry or white wine if desired. Serve over corn bread, pastry shells, toast or rice. Or bake in Rice Crust at 350° 40 minutes.

Heat white meat; serve over bread, top with gravy. Add mashed potatoes and a scoop of dressing, if desired.

Heat in canned cream of celery soup; add sautéed onion, cooked peas. Serve over biscuits seasoned with ¼ teaspoon curry powder.

Turkey Balls: Grind and mix with eggs, bread, and seasonings to taste. Shape into balls, roll in bread crumbs, and fry in hot oil.

BAKED TURKEY-CHEESE SANDWICH

1 *cup cooked turkey, chopped*
¼ *cup celery, chopped*
3 *tablespoons mayonnaise*
1½ *teaspoons onion, finely chopped*
1 *teaspoon lemon juice*
   Salt and pepper to taste
2 *hamburger buns, split, toasted, and buttered (or 4 slices bread)*
2 *slices mild cheese*

In small bowl combine turkey, celery, mayonnaise, onion, lemon juice, salt, and pepper. Spread on toasted buns. Top with cheese. Broil or heat in 300° oven until cheese melts. Makes 4 open-face sandwiches.

TANGY TURKEY SALAD

4 *cups cooked macaroni*
3 *cups cooked turkey, cubed*
1 *carrot, grated*
1 *cup celery, diced*
1 *medium onion, diced*
½ *cup radishes, sliced*
½ *cup green peppers, diced*
½ *cup green olives, sliced*
½ *cup parsley, chopped*
1 *cup cooked peas, if desired*
1½ *cups cubed cheese, if desired*

Dressing:
1½ *cups mayonnaise*
¼ *cup lemon juice*
½ *cup sugar*
1 *teaspoon salt*
⅛ *teaspoon pepper*
1 *teaspoon seasoned salt*

In large bowl toss macaroni, turkey, vegetables, and cheese, if used. In separate bowl blend mayonnaise, lemon juice, sugar, salt, pepper, and seasoned salt. Pour over salad and blend well. Chill several hours or overnight. Serves 10.

TURKEY-CORN CHOWDER

¼ pound bacon, diced
1 cup onion, chopped
3 cups raw potatoes, diced
1 cup celery, diced
½ teaspoon salt
⅛ teaspoon pepper
6 cups chicken or turkey broth
1 (16-ounce) can cream-style corn
1 (13-ounce) can evaporated milk
1½ cups cooked turkey, diced
½ teaspoon marjoram
½ teaspoon thyme

In large saucepan sauté bacon until crisp; remove from pan. Sauté onion in bacon fat until soft. Add potatoes, celery, salt, pepper, broth, and bacon; cover and simmer 20 minutes or until potatoes are tender. Stir in corn, milk, turkey, and seasonings. Heat until warmed through. Serves 6.

TURKEY HASH

½ cup onion, minced
2 tablespoons butter
½ cup canned mushrooms, if desired
2 cups cooked turkey, cubed
1 to 2 cups cooked potato, cubed
1½ teaspoons seasoned salt
     Dash pepper
⅔ cup milk, light cream, or evaporated milk

In medium saucepan sauté onion in butter until tender. Stir in mushrooms, turkey, potato, salt, and pepper. Add milk and stir gently to mix. Heat until warmed through. Serves 4.

TURKEY-PINEAPPLE CURRY

½ cup onion, chopped
⅓ cup butter or margarine
⅓ cup flour
1 teaspoon curry powder
1 teaspoon salt
4 cups turkey or chicken broth
3 cups cooked turkey, cubed
1 cup pineapple tidbits, drained
     Hot cooked rice

(Prepare in advance and reheat, if possible.) In large skillet sauté onion in butter until soft. Blend in flour, curry powder, and salt. Add broth; cook over low heat, stirring constantly until thickened. Add turkey and pineapple; heat until warmed through. Serve over hot rice with desired curry accompaniments. Serves 6.

TURKEY NEWBURG

> 4 slices corn bread or corn muffins
> 3 tablespoons butter or margarine
> 3 tablespoons flour
> 1½ cups light cream
> ¼ cup sliced canned mushrooms with liquid
> 1 chicken bouillon cube
>   Dash pepper
> ½ teaspoon chervil
> 1 tablespoon parsley, chopped
> 1 tablespoon pimiento, chopped
> 2 to 4 tablespoons dry sherry
> 8 slices cooked turkey, warmed

In medium saucepan melt butter. Stir in flour. Blend in cream and mushroom liquid. Add crumbled bouillon cube, pepper, and chervil. Cook, stirring constantly until mixture thickens. Add parsley, pimiento, mushrooms, and sherry; heat gently. Cut corn bread or muffins horizontally; butter if desired. Place turkey slices over corn bread halves; top with sauce. Serves 4.

CREAMED TURKEY PAPRIKASH

> ½ cup onion, sliced
> 3 tablespoons butter or margarine
> 2 tablespoons flour
> 2 teaspoons paprika
> ½ teaspoon salt
> 1 cup turkey or chicken broth
> 2 egg yolks, slightly beaten
> 1 cup dairy sour cream
> 2 cups cooked turkey, cubed
> ½ cup canned mushrooms, drained
> 4 ounces egg noodles, cooked

In medium saucepan sauté onion in butter until tender; blend in flour, paprika, and salt. Add broth; cook and stir until mixture thickens. Continue cooking 1 minute more. Combine a small amount of sauce with egg yolks, then stir egg yolks into saucepan and continue cooking 1 minute. Add turkey and mushrooms. Heat just until warmed. Remove from heat and stir in sour cream. Serve over noodles. Serves 4.

TURKEY DIVAN CASSEROLE

2½ cups chopped broccoli, cooked and drained
2 tablespoons butter
2 tablespoons flour
½ teaspoon salt
2 cups milk
½ cup Swiss cheese, shredded
2 cups cooked turkey, sliced
½ cup soft bread crumbs
¼ cup grated Parmesan cheese
1 tablespoon butter, melted

Arrange broccoli in 7-by-11-inch baking dish. In medium saucepan melt 2 tablespoons butter; blend in flour and salt. Add milk; cook, stirring constantly until mixture thickens. Remove from heat; add Swiss cheese and stir until melted. Add turkey slices. Spoon mixture over broccoli. Combine bread crumbs, Parmesan cheese, and melted butter; sprinkle over top. Bake at 350° 20 to 25 minutes. Serves 6.

TURKEY TETRAZZINI CASSEROLE

1 to 2 cups cooked turkey, diced
1 tablespoon butter
1 tablespoon flour
¼ teaspoon instant chicken bouillon
1 egg yolk
1 cup milk
¼ teaspoon salt
1 cup cooked spaghetti or egg noodles
¼ cup mushrooms, sliced
1 tablespoon green pepper, diced
1 tablespoon lemon juice
1 tablespoon grated Parmesan cheese
2 tablespoons slivered almonds
Dash pepper

In medium saucepan melt butter; add flour, salt, and pepper, and blend. Stir in chicken bouillon; cook until smooth. Combine milk and egg yolk in separate bowl; add mixture to saucepan. Heat, stirring constantly, until mixture is thickened. Add spaghetti, mushrooms, green pepper, turkey, and lemon juice. Place in 1½-quart greased baking dish. Sprinkle with Parmesan cheese and almonds. Bake at 350° 30 to 40 minutes. Serves 2 or 3.

EGGS

EGGS, HARD-COOKED

How to Use: Slice or quarter and use as garnish; use alone or on lettuce leaves.

Chop and add to sandwich spreads.

Deviled Eggs: Mix 6 mashed egg yolks, ½ teaspoon salt, ¼ teaspoon pepper, 1 teaspoon prepared mustard, and 4 tablespoons mayonnaise. Mound mixture into halves of egg whites.

Add chopped eggs to fish and meat sauces.

Sieve yolks and sprinkle over fish, soups, salads.

Egg-salad sandwich spread: Mix chopped eggs with minced onion, prepared mustard, salt and pepper to taste, and moisten with mayonnaise.

Add chopped eggs to tossed salads.

Seafood-egg sandwich filling: Combine flaked tuna or salmon, minced celery, onion salt, and salad dressing. Serve on bread or heap on greens and serve as salad.

Add to Chicken à la King.

Eggs à la King: Fold sliced or quartered eggs into a medium white sauce; add mushrooms, diced pimiento, diced ham or flaked tuna, if desired. Serve over toast points, chow mein noodles, or hot biscuits.

TANGY BAKED EGG CASSEROLE

> 6 *hard-cooked eggs, sliced*
> ½ *cup mayonnaise*
> ½ *cup catsup*
> 1 *teaspoon lemon juice*
> ¼ *cup milk*
> ½ *teaspoon salt*
> *Chopped parsley*
> *Hot cooked rice or toast*

Meat, Poultry, Fish, Eggs, and Beans **55**

Arrange egg slices in an 8- or 9-inch buttered baking dish. Combine mayonnaise, catsup, lemon juice, milk, and salt; stir until smooth. Spread mixture over eggs. Bake at 350° 15 minutes. Top with parsley. Serve over rice or toast. Serves 4.

EGGS, SCRAMBLED

How to Use: Break up in small pieces with fork and add to soups, salads, and white sauces, or sprinkle over cooked spinach.

Combine with chopped cooked bacon or minced ham to make a sandwich spread.

Add to cheese sauces.

EGG WHITES, RAW

How to Use: Add to omelets, scrambled eggs, and egg foo yong before cooking.

Add to French-toast egg mixture.

Poach egg whites. Chop and add to egg salad, casseroles, cheese sauce, tossed salads.

Whip raw egg white into salad dressings. Use at once; do not store leftovers.

Add up to 4 egg whites to meat or fish loaf, hamburger patties, timbales, or croquettes. If mixture gets too moist, add bread crumbs.

Add to blender drinks made of milk and fruits or fruit juices. Sweeten to taste with honey.

Use in chiffon cakes, silver cakes, sunshine cakes, loaf cakes, angel-food cakes, white butter cakes.

Use in meringues, Baked Alaska desserts, macaroons, boiled cake icings, 7-minute icing, dessert soufflés, Floating Island dessert, Angel Pie.

Use in frozen desserts and fruit whips.

Add to malted milk drinks or ice cream floats.

To freeze egg whites, pour 1½ tablespoons of raw egg whites into ice cube tray units. Or place desired number of whites in freezer containers, allowing ½-inch head space. Cover and freeze. Will keep four months. Thaw in unopened container in refrigerator or at room temperature. Whites will whip to larger volume if allowed to reach room temperature before using.

EGG YOLKS, RAW

How to Use: Poach and use as hard-cooked egg: Add to salads or sandwich fillings, or sieve and use as garnish for canapés, soups, creamed fish, or cooked green vegetables.

Add to scrambled eggs before cooking.

Use in homemade noodles.

Use in Hollandaise, Béarnaise, Mornay, or Newburg sauces.

Use to thicken cream sauces, à la King sauces.

Use to make homemade mayonnaise.

1 egg yolk can be added to recipes for meat loaf, white sauce, cheese sauce, beer-cheese soup, pancakes, muffins, cookies, or pudding.

2 egg yolks can be added to recipes for pancakes, waffles, French toast, or cream soups (mix egg yolk with milk before adding to soup).

Substitute 2 egg yolks for 1 whole egg in custards, salad dressings, cream pie fillings, scalloped corn.

Substitute 2 yolks plus 1 teaspoon water for 1 whole egg in cookies and yeast doughs.

Use in eggnogs, yellow cakes, sponge cakes, spritz cookies, baked custards.

Some cake fillings and puddings call for egg yolks.

Use in custard sauces, rum sauces, Zabaglione or Sabayon sauces.

To freeze egg yolks, mix yolks gently, add either 1 teaspoon salt or 2 teaspoons sugar for each cup of yolks, depending on whether eggs will be used for sweet or salted dishes. Pour into freezer containers. If desired, yolks may be frozen in plastic ice cube trays. To thaw, keep in covered container and thaw at room temperature. 1 tablespoon defrosted egg yolk equals 1 yolk.

BLENDER HOLLANDAISE SAUCE

3 *egg yolks*
2 *tablespoons lemon juice*
½ *teaspoon salt*
    Pinch cayenne pepper
½ *cup butter, melted*

Place egg yolks, lemon juice, salt, and cayenne pepper in blender container. Blend on low speed just until mixed. Cover blender; turn on low speed and slowly pour one-third of the butter through opening in blender cover. Turn blender to high speed and slowly pour in remaining butter. Blend until smooth and thickened. Serve over cooked asparagus, broccoli, or other green vegetables. Makes 1 cup.

SOFT CUSTARD SAUCE

¾ cup sugar
⅛ teaspoon salt
1½ cups scalded milk
4 egg yolks, beaten (or 2 whole eggs)
2 tablespoons butter, if desired
1 teaspoon vanilla

In top of double boiler combine all ingredients except butter and vanilla; cook over hot, not boiling, water, stirring constantly, until mixture coats spoon. Remove from heat. Stir in butter, if desired, and vanilla. Chill before serving. Serve over fruit cakes, puddings, or Trifle. Serves 4.

FISH

How to Use: Add to salads and aspics.
Use in chef's salads.
Use in sandwich spreads.
Add to omelets, scrambled eggs, or soufflés; flavor with lemon juice, onion, green pepper, or dill.
Combine with celery, cucumber, onion, parsley, lemon juice, and mayonnaise; season to taste and use to stuff raw tomatoes or green peppers.
Add to chowders, soups, and bisques.
Use in Jambalaya.
Serve cold fish fillets topped with mayonnaise flavored with tarragon, dill, thyme, or parsley. Chill herbed mayonnaise before using.

FISH CHOWDER

2 cups fish, cooked and flaked
2 slices bacon, cooked and drained
½ cup onion, finely chopped
2 cups potatoes, cooked and cubed
1 teaspoon salt

Pepper to taste
¼ cup butter or margarine
1¼ cups evaporated milk

Chowder tastes best when made ahead, refrigerated, and reheated. Combine all ingredients and heat until thoroughly warmed. Thin, if desired, with milk or broth. Season to taste. Serves 6.

FISH BISQUE

1 slice bacon, diced
¼ cup green pepper, chopped
½ cup onion, chopped
½ cup carrots, diced
1 cup chopped fresh vegetables, if desired
½ clove garlic, minced
Dill seeds or dill weed to taste
1 cup fish or vegetable broth
1 cup fish, cooked and flaked
Salt and pepper to taste

In medium saucepan with cover sauté bacon, vegetables, and garlic. When vegetables are almost tender add strained broth and dill. Heat to boiling, then simmer until vegetables are done. Season to taste with salt and pepper. Just before serving add fish. Serves 3 or 4.

BAKED FISH LOAF

2 cups fish, cooked and flaked
1 egg
¼ cup evaporated milk
¾ cup soft bread crumbs
½ teaspoon salt
¼ teaspoon paprika
1 tablespoon vegetable oil
3 tablespoons parsley, minced
2 tablespoons celery, chopped
2 tablespoons onion, chopped
2 tablespoons green pepper, chopped
2 teaspoons lemon juice

Combine all ingredients and place in greased loaf pan. Bake at 400° for 30 to 40 minutes. Serve hot with white sauce or cheese sauce. May be served cold also. Serves 4.

FISH CROQUETTES

2 *cups fish, cooked and flaked*
1 *cup thick white sauce*
1 *egg*
2 *tablespoons onion, minced*
2 *tablespoons parsley, chopped*
1 *teaspoon dill seed, if desired*
  Salt and pepper to taste
  Crumbs for breading

Combine all ingredients except crumbs. Shape into croquettes, roll in crumbs, and bake at 350° for 20 minutes; or if desired, sauté in fry pan in vegetable oil. If desired, make 2 cups of white sauce; use 1 cup in recipe and save second cup to serve over croquettes. Add up to 1 cup cooked vegetables, if desired, to topping. Serves 4.

QUICK FISH SALAD

2 *cups fish, cooked and flaked*
1 *cucumber, diced*
¼ *cup celery, minced*
2 *tablespoons pimiento, chopped*
¼ *cup onion, chopped*
¼ *teaspoon salt*
  Dash pepper
2 *tablespoons lemon juice*
¼ *cup mayonnaise*
1 *to 2 cups cooked macaroni shells, if desired*
  Lettuce leaves

In medium bowl combine all ingredients except lettuce leaves. Chill and serve on lettuce. Serves 4.

SARDINES

How to Use: Sardine Dip: Add sardines to cream cheese thinned with lemon juice. Add chopped parsley, paprika, chives, and pimiento.

Sardine Butter Spread: Blend 6 tablespoons softened butter, 1 teaspoon lemon juice, ¼ teaspoon prepared mustard, and ¼ teaspoon Worcestershire. Add 1 small can of sardines, skinned, deboned, drained, and mashed. Blend well. Egg salad goes well in combination with this mixture.

Sandwich Spread: Mix sardines with a little catsup, lemon juice, and chopped pimiento or olives.

LEGUMES

BAKED BEANS

How to Use: Spread on buttered bread as sandwich filling.

Mash beans and spread on ham loaf or meat loaf before baking.

Add to bean soups, Cassoulet.

Add spoonful of warmed beans to top of cooked hamburger patties. Surround with green pepper ring, if desired.

Broiled Bean Sandwich: Spread mashed beans on bread that has been spread with butter and prepared mustard. Sprinkle shredded sharp cheese over beans. Broil until cheese melts.

Grilled Bean-Cheese Sandwich: Mash 1 cup baked beans; add 2 tablespoons catsup, 2 teaspoons prepared mustard, 1 tablespoon minced onion, 1 tablespoon brown sugar; add to beans and mix well. Spread bean mixture on bread. Top with slices of cheddar cheese and a second slice of bread. Butter both slices of bread on the outside. Sauté in skillet until golden brown. Makes 4 sandwiches.

Hot Beans and Franks Sandwich: Sauté sliced frankfurters and chopped onion in butter until onion is tender. Add baked beans, a little prepared mustard, and catsup; heat until warmed through. Serve on toasted sandwich buns.

BAKED BEAN AND TOMATO SOUP

2 *cups baked beans*
3 *cups water*
1 *small onion, sliced*
1 *(16-ounce) can tomatoes*
1½ *tablespoons butter or margarine*
1½ *tablespoons flour*
  Salt and pepper to taste

In large saucepan combine beans, water, onions, and tomatoes. Cook over medium heat for 20 minutes. Put through sieve or puree in blender. Set mixture aside. In same saucepan, melt butter; add flour and heat to bubbling.

Add a small amount of the pureed bean mixture to saucepan; heat and stir. Add remaining bean mixture. Salt and pepper to taste. Simmer 5 minutes before serving. Serves 6.

BAKED BEAN SANDWICH SPREAD

1 *cup baked beans, mashed*
¼ *cup celery, minced*
1 *tablespoon onion, chopped*
Mayonnaise

Drain excess liquid, if any, from beans. In medium bowl combine beans, celery, and onion. Add enough mayonnaise to moisten to desired consistency for spreading. Serves 2 or 3.

KIDNEY BEANS

How to Use: Add to Welsh Rarebit.
Mix drained beans with mild cheese, chopped onion, salt, and taco sauce; mound in avocado halves brushed with lemon juice. Place on lettuce leaves and serve with corn chips.
See also "Other Dried Beans" section.

BEAN AND BACON CASSEROLE

2 *cups kidney beans, cooked and drained*
1 *cup canned tomatoes*
¼ *cup onion, chopped*
¼ *pound raw bacon, chopped*
1 *cup grated cheese*

In a medium-size greased baking dish, layer beans, bacon, and onions; repeat layers. Pour tomatoes over layers. Top with grated cheese. Bake at 350° 45 to 60 minutes. Serves 4 to 6.

THREE-BEAN SALAD

2 *cups cooked green beans*
2 *cups cooked wax beans*
2 *cups cooked kidney beans*
1 *small onion, sliced*
1 *green pepper, chopped*
¾ *cup sugar*
⅓ *cup vegetable oil*
⅔ *cup vinegar*
1 *teaspoon salt*
    Pepper to taste

In large dish or jar with tight-fitting cover, combine all ingredients. Chill at least 4 hours before serving. Serves 6 to 8.

LIMA BEANS

How to Use: Heat in tomato soup.

Combine with equal parts cooked whole-kernel corn; add butter or cream and heat gently.

Combine with cooked celery, carrots, or tomatoes for a mixed vegetable dish.

Prepare like Creole Green Beans.

Squash Stuffing: Mix cooked lima beans with sour cream and chives and heat gently. Serve it on baked winter squash halves.

See also "Other Dried Beans" section.

OTHER DRIED BEANS (PINTO, NAVY, GARBANZO, ETC.)

How to Use: Add to vegetable soups.

Substitute for black-eyed peas in Hopping John.

Mix in baking dish with corn, canned tomatoes, salt, brown sugar, onion, and paprika. Top with crumbs and bake until heated through.

Bean Salad: Combine with French dressing, season with onion, sweet pickles, or curry powder. Add other raw vegetables, if desired. Chill and serve on lettuce leaves.

MINESTRONE

1 *onion, chopped*
2 *stalks celery, chopped*
1 *sliced zucchini, if desired*
   Up to 3 cups chopped cooked or raw vegetables, if desired
1 *clove garlic, minced*
1½ *tablespoons vegetable oil*
1 *(6-ounce) can tomato paste plus 1 cup water, or 2 cups
   cooked tomatoes, chopped*
¼ *teaspoon basil*
¼ *teaspoon oregano*
3 *cups meat or vegetable broth*
3 *cups cooked dried beans*
   Up to 1 cup cooked spaghetti or macaroni
   Up to 1 cup cooked meat, diced
   Salt and pepper to taste
   Grated Parmesan cheese

In large saucepan sauté onion, celery, zucchini, other vegetables, if desired, and garlic in oil. Add tomatoes and simmer 10 minutes. Add basil, oregano, broth, and beans; cook 15 minutes, stirring frequently. Add meat and spaghetti; heat through. Add salt and pepper to taste. Sprinkle with Parmesan cheese before serving. Serves 6 to 8.

HAMBURGER-BEAN SKILLET

1 *pound ground beef*
1 *medium onion, chopped*
3 *cups cooked dried beans*
3 *cups cooked tomatoes*
1 *teaspoon salt*
1 *bay leaf*
1 *teaspoon oregano*
2 *tablespoons parsley, chopped*

In large skillet with cover sauté ground beef and onions until beef has lost its red color; drain off excess fat. Add remaining ingredients. Cover and simmer 15 minutes. Serves 6.

Vegetables

ARTICHOKES, GLOBE

How to Use: Trim off tough bottom row of leaves. Cut off thorn part of leaves with scissors. Steam until tender, about 45 minutes. Serve one artichoke per person. Pluck off an individual leaf. Dip base of leaf in melted butter, mayonnaise, or Hollandaise sauce. Scrape soft pulp from base of leaf with teeth; discard remainder of leaf. Cut the inside core with a knife and fork, dipping pieces in sauce. (Do not eat the fuzzy globe surrounding the artichoke heart.)

Artichokes may be stuffed for a main dish. The preparation is elaborate; consult a specialty cookbook.

ASPARAGUS, COOKED

How to Use: Add to tossed salads.

Salad ideas: Marinate asparagus in French dressing and serve on lettuce leaves with tomato wedges, hard-cooked eggs, and chicken or seafood salad; or serve on lettuce with pimiento strips and pieces of cooked bacon.

Use in aspics.

Use as garnish for salad plates. Asparagus spears may be placed in a green pepper ring or on lemon or lime slices.

Add to cream sauces and cream soups.

Asparagus soup: Heat asparagus in chicken broth seasoned with onion, parsley, salt, and pepper. Puree in blender. Heat again and add cream mixed with egg yolks. Heat and stir until slightly thickened; do not let boil.

Roll up spears in thin slices of boiled ham, fasten with

wooden pick, and top with cheese sauce and bread crumbs. Bake at 375° for 20 minutes or until heated through.

Baked asparagus dishes: Place asparagus in shallow baking dish, spread with mayonnaise, sprinkle with shredded cheddar cheese, and brown under broiler until topping is bubbly; or top with grated Parmesan cheese and melted butter and bake at 450° for 5 to 10 minutes; or cover asparagus with slices of hard-cooked egg, a thick white sauce, and buttered crumbs and bake at 350° for 30 minutes.

BEETS

How to Use: Use in Borscht.

Serve small cooked beets whole or sliced on salad greens.

Slice large cooked cold beets and serve topped with cole slaw or Russian salad.

Marinate cooked sliced beets in French dressing. Add sliced onions if desired. Before serving drain and mix with dairy sour cream.

Mix chopped cooked beets with parsley, chives, and dairy sour cream.

Combine chopped cooked beets with sliced or chopped hard-cooked eggs and mayonnaise.

Heat cooked beets in dairy sour cream; add a small amount of onion, horseradish, salt, and chives. Heat in double boiler.

Add chopped cooked beets to corned beef hash.

Bake cooked beets with apple and onion slices, salt, nutmeg, and butter. Heat in covered baking dish at 350° until apples and onions are tender.

Bake cooked beets in orange sauce. To make orange sauce, combine 2 tablespoons melted butter, 2 tablespoons flour, ¼ cup sugar, and ½ cup orange juice. Bake in covered dish at 350° 15 minutes. Serve with roast pork, poultry, or game.

HARVARD BEETS

2 *tablespoons butter*
1 *tablespoon cornstarch*
¼ *cup sugar*
   Dash pepper
1 *teaspoon salt*

⅓ cup vinegar
2 to 3 cups beets, cooked (reserve liquid)

In medium saucepan melt butter. Add cornstarch, sugar, salt, and pepper; blend well. Add vinegar; cook over moderate heat until thick. Add beets with liquid and continue to cook over moderate heat until warmed through. Serves 4 to 6.

BROCCOLI

How to Use: Cut raw broccoli into thin slices or flowerets for dipping.

Slice raw broccoli very thin and stir-fry with seasoned beef. Serve over rice.

Use cooked broccoli spears as a base for creamed vegetables or creamed seafood.

Top cooked spears with sauce made of cream soup, sautéed onions, and grated Parmesan cheese. Thin sauce with milk to desired consistency.

Use cooked chopped broccoli spears as you would cooked potatoes in main-dish salads; combine broccoli pieces with desired combinations of hard-cooked eggs, cheese, canned tuna, radishes, celery, green peppers, carrots, onions, parsley, pickles, chives, and fried bacon. Season with salt and pepper. Moisten with mayonnaise or salad dressing.

Use in Chicken or Turkey Divan.

BROCCOLI-CORN CASSEROLE

1 (10-ounce) package frozen chopped broccoli or 1½ cups
    fresh broccoli, chopped
1 (16-ounce) can cream-style corn
¼ cup Saltine cracker crumbs
1 egg, beaten
2 tablespoons butter, melted
1 tablespoon instant minced onion
½ teaspoon salt
    Dash pepper
¼ cup Saltine cracker crumbs
2 tablespoons butter, melted

Cook and drain broccoli. In 1½-quart casserole combine broccoli, corn, ¼ cup cracker crumbs, egg, 2 tablespoons melted butter, onion, salt, and pepper. Blend ¼ cup cracker crumbs and 2 tablespoons melted butter; sprinkle over vegetables. Bake, uncovered, at 350° for 35 to 45 minutes. Serves 6.

BRUSSELS SPROUTS

How to Use: Cook sprouts in a small amount of beef or chicken broth with minced onion. Season to taste with salt, pepper, lemon juice, and butter.

Steam fresh or frozen thawed sprouts in butter. When tender-crisp add a little lemon juice. Season with salt and pepper. Add dairy sour cream and heat gently.

Combine cooked sprouts with any combination of onions, peas, green or wax beans, and celery.

Place cooked sprouts and chopped cooked egg whites in a thick cream sauce. Serve over toast, garnished with sieved cooked egg yolks and parsley sprigs or with crisp bacon or toasted almonds.

Baked Brussels Sprouts: Bake cooked sprouts in tomato sauce, sprinkled with grated cheese. Bake at 350° 15 minutes.

COMPANY BRUSSELS SPROUTS

1 (10¾-ounce) can cream of celery soup
½ cup milk
½ cup celery, diced
2½ cups Brussels sprouts, cooked
½ cup grated cheese
1 tablespoon pimiento, chopped
½ cup slivered almonds, if desired
½ cup crumbs for topping

In ovenproof skillet mix soup and milk. Add celery; simmer until celery is barely tender. Add Brussels sprouts, cheese, pimiento, and nuts. Cover with crumbs. Bake at 350° 20 minutes or until mixture bubbles. Serves 4 to 6.

BRUSSELS SPROUTS RELISH

3 cups Brussels sprouts
¼ cup wine vinegar
¼ teaspoon salt

½ teaspoon dry mustard
¾ cup vegetable oil
  Pepper to taste
1 tablespoon green onions, minced
¾ teaspoon dried dill weed
¼ cup dairy sour cream
  Radish roses for garnish

Steam Brussels sprouts. Remove loose outer leaves. Combine vinegar, salt, mustard, oil, pepper, onions, and dill weed. Place sprouts in a large dish with tight-fitting cover. Pour dressing over sprouts. Chill several hours or overnight. Drain dressing before serving and mix the green sprouts with sour cream. Place in serving dish. Sprinkle with additional dill weed, if desired. Garnish with radish roses. Serves 10 to 12.

CABBAGE

CELERY CABBAGE (CHINESE CABBAGE)

How to Use: Shred and use raw in salads as you would use lettuce.
> Cut in crosswise sections and serve as salad with a sweet French dressing.
> Shred and sauté in butter.
> Add to stir-fried meat.
> Substitute for spinach in many recipes calling for cooked spinach.

GREEN CABBAGE

How to Use: For salads, shred cabbage and mix with desired combination of shredded carrots, diced green pepper, pineapple chunks, apple or pear slices, raisins, dates, toasted nuts, and so on. Add dressing of dairy sour cream thinned with fruit juice, or French dressing, or mayonnaise mixed with fruit juice or chutney.
> Add to soups, pot roasts, stews, and boiled dinners.
> Serve as accompaniment to corned beef hash.
> Steam and serve with white sauce or cheese sauce.
> Sauté in butter or bacon drippings with sliced celery, green pepper, onions, and tomatoes. Steam until tender. Season to taste with salt, pepper, and sugar.
> Parboil and stuff with hash or ground beef-rice mixture.

CABBAGE SLAW

5 *cups cabbage, shredded*
1 *teaspoon salt*
¼ *teaspoon celery seed*
⅔ *cup sugar*
½ *cup vinegar*
½ *cup water*
⅓ *cup vegetable oil*
1½ *tablespoons onion, minced*

Mix all ingredients together. Place in container with airtight lid. Chill several hours before serving. Salad will keep several days in refrigerator. Makes 10 servings.

QUICK CREAMY COLESLAW

1 *small head cabbage, shredded*
2 *tablespoons onion, chopped, or 1 teaspoon instant minced onion*
1 *tablespoon sugar*
½ *teaspoon salt*
½ *cup mayonnaise*
1 *tablespoon vinegar*
Dash pepper

In small bowl combine onion, sugar, salt, mayonnaise, vinegar, and pepper; let stand while shredding cabbage. Pour dressing over cabbage and toss to coat cabbage completely. Serve at once. Serves 6 to 8.

SWEET-SOUR SKILLET SLAW

2 *slices bacon, drained and crumbled (reserve bacon drippings)*
4 *tablespoons onion, chopped*
2 *tablespoons vinegar*
2 *tablespoons water*
1 *tablespoon sugar*
½ *teaspoon salt*
Dash pepper
4 *cups cabbage, shredded*
1 *medium apple, pared and chopped*

In medium saucepan sauté onion in bacon drippings. Stir in vinegar, water, sugar, salt, and pepper; bring to boiling. Add cabbage and apple; toss gently. Cover and cook over medium heat 5 minutes. Top with bacon before serving. Serves 4 to 6.

VEGETABLE SKILLET SLAW

> ¼ cup butter or margarine
> 2 cups cabbage, coarsely shredded
> ⅔ cup celery, cut on diagonal
> ⅔ cup carrot, thinly sliced
> ¼ cup green pepper, slivered
> ¼ cup onion, chopped
> 1 teaspoon salt
> Dash pepper

In medium skillet, melt butter. Add vegetables, salt, and pepper. Cover and cook over medium heat until vegetables are barely tender. Garnish with parsley if desired. Serve at once. Serves 4 to 6.

CABBAGE-HAMBURGER BAKE

> 1 pound ground beef
> 1 small onion, chopped
> ¼ cup uncooked rice
> Salt and pepper to taste
> 1 small head cabbage
> 2 cups spaghetti sauce

In large skillet brown meat, onion, rice, salt, and pepper. Drain excess drippings. In greased 2½-quart baking dish layer cabbage leaves, torn into 1-inch bits, meat-rice mixture, and spaghetti sauce. Bake, covered, at 350° for 40 to 45 minutes. Serves 4.

PURPLE CABBAGE

How to Use: Add small amounts of shredded cabbage to tossed salads and vegetable soups.

Shred and moisten with seasoned mayonnaise; toss and top with crumbled cooked bacon.

Sauté shredded cabbage and chopped onion in bacon drippings. Add salt and pepper to taste. If desired, add red wine, diced apples, brown sugar, or vinegar. Cover and cook until tender, 35 to 45 minutes.

Shred one head cabbage; place in saucepan along with ¼ cup each currant jelly and red wine vinegar. Cover tightly and cook 45 to 55 minutes over medium heat until tender. Salt and pepper to taste.

CARROTS

How to Use: Cut raw carrots into sticks or curls to use as nibblers. Thin carrot sticks may be stuffed through pitted ripe olives for an attractive hors d'oeuvre.

Carrot garnish: Cut carrots into crosswise sections and remove center core; slip sprig of parsley or watercress through center opening.

Shred and add to cole slaw.

Shred or grate raw carrots and add to lemon-flavored gelatin along with desired fruits or vegetables.

Grate carrots and mix with raisins or chopped walnuts and crushed pineapple. Moisten with mayonnaise or dairy sour cream, if desired.

Marinated Carrot Relish: Combine 4 cups sliced carrots, 1 chopped green pepper, 1 chopped onion, and salt and pepper with 1 cup vinaigrette sauce. Chill several hours before using.

Carrot Relish: Grate 2 cups of carrots; mix with 2 ground-up lemons with rind, and ¾ cup sugar. Cover and refrigerate two days before using.

Cook carrots in chicken broth seasoned with butter, salt, pepper, and sugar. Add lemon juice and parsley before serving.

Combine cooked carrots with cooked peas. Season with salt, butter, and pepper to taste.

Mashed Carrots: Cook 1 pound carrots in water until tender. Drain, reserving cooking water. In small skillet melt 1 tablespoon butter; add 1 tablespoon flour and sauté until lightly browned. Add to carrots and stir. Blend in enough cooking water to make carrots the consistency of mashed potatoes.

Golden Glow Potatoes: Add hot cooked carrots to equal amount of hot cooked potatoes; mash potatoes and carrots. Add butter, salt, and pepper to taste. Thin to desired consistency with milk.

Sweet Skillet Carrots: Cook carrots in small amount of water until tender. Season with salt. Add desired combinations of butter, honey or sugar, cinnamon, nutmeg, or ginger. Cook 3 minutes after adding seasonings.

Sweet Baked Carrots: Scrub carrots; peel or leave skins on, as desired. Place carrots in a baking dish with cover; dot lightly with butter and sprinkle with brown sugar. Cover and bake at 350° 1 hour.

Tangy Baked Carrots: Sauté 1 small onion or 4 green onions in butter in an ovenproof skillet until tender. Add 1 pound carrots, minced parsley, salt and pepper to taste, and ¼ cup light cream. Cover and bake at 350° 1 hour.

Use in Carrot Cake.

VEGETABLE SALAD MOLD

1 (3-ounce) package lemon gelatin
¾ teaspoon salt
   Dash pepper
2 tablespoons vinegar
2 teaspoons grated onion
½ cup celery, diced
½ cup carrots, minced
½ cup green pepper, minced
½ cup raw cabbage, chopped fine

Prepare gelatin as directed. Pour into medium bowl or 4-cup mold. Add salt, pepper, and vinegar. Chill until slightly thickened; fold in vegetables. Chill until set. Serves 6.

CARROT BARS

2 eggs
1 cup sugar
¾ cup vegetable oil
1¼ cups flour
1 teaspoon cinnamon
1 teaspoon baking soda
¼ teaspoon salt
1 teaspoon vanilla
¾ cup carrots, cooked and mashed
½ cup nuts, chopped

In large bowl beat eggs until light. Add sugar and mix well. Combine flour, cinnamon, soda, and salt. Add oil and dry ingredients alternately to egg mixture. Add vanilla. Fold in carrots and nuts. Spread in greased 9-by-13-

inch pan. Bake at 350° 25 to 30 minutes. Cool and frost with cream cheese frosting.

CAULIFLOWER

How to Use: Break into flowerets and eat raw, alone or with dips.

Slice thinly and add to tossed green salads.

Add cooked cauliflowerets to tossed or molded vegetable salads.

Marinated Cooked Cauliflower: Cover with French or Italian dressing. Chill before serving.

Cook in ½ cup salted water in covered pan until tender; drain and add cream sauce, cheese sauce, or a cream soup or tomato soup. Add color by adding diced pimiento or green pepper, bacon, or toasted chopped nuts.

Cauliflower Vegetable Platter: Use a whole cooked cauliflower as the center for a vegetable platter. Surround cauliflower with cooked carrots and broccoli spears. Cover with cheese sauce. Garnish with chopped pimiento and parsley.

CAULIFLOWER-BEAN SALAD

3 cups cauliflower, chopped
2 cups kidney beans, cooked and drained
4 green onions, chopped
2 tablespoons green chilies, chopped
2 tomatoes, peeled and chopped

Dressing:
½ cup vegetable oil
¼ cup wine vinegar
2 cloves garlic, minced
1 teaspoon salt
½ teaspoon sugar
½ teaspoon pepper
¼ teaspoon cumin

In medium saucepan boil cauliflower in salted water 1 minute; drain. In medium bowl with cover combine cauliflower, kidney beans, green onions, and chilies. In small bowl combine oil, vinegar, garlic, salt, sugar, pepper, and cumin; pour dressing over vegetables and toss gently. Cover and refrigerate several hours. Just before serving add tomatoes and toss. Serve on salad greens, if desired. Serves 6 to 8.

CAULIFLOWER-BACON TOSSED SALAD

1 *head of lettuce, torn into bite-size pieces*
1 *onion, thinly sliced*
1 *pound bacon, cut in 1-inch pieces, fried crisp and drained*
1 *head cauliflower, broken into small flowerets*
¼ *cup sugar*
⅓ *cup Parmesan cheese, grated*
   Salt and pepper to taste
2 *cups mayonnaise*

Layer lettuce, onion, bacon, and cauliflower in large bowl. Sprinkle with sugar, Parmesan cheese, salt, and pepper. Spread mayonnaise over all. Cover and refrigerate several hours. Just before serving toss well. Serves 10 to 12.

REFRIGERATOR PICKLED CAULIFLOWER

1 *head cauliflower, separated into flowerets*
1 *cup vegetable oil*
½ *cup cider vinegar*
1 *rib celery with leaves, sliced thin*
½ *cup onion, chopped*
1 *slice lemon*
1 *clove garlic, minced*
1 *teaspoon salt*
4 *peppercorns*
1 *bay leaf*
⅓ *cup pimiento, chopped*

Cook cauliflower in salted water 10 minutes; drain and place in 1½-quart container with cover. In saucepan combine oil, vinegar, celery, onion, lemon, garlic, salt, peppercorns, and bay leaf; bring to boil and pour over cauliflower. Gently toss in pimiento. Cover and chill. Serves 10 to 12.

CAULIFLOWER SOUP

1 *medium cauliflower, cut up*
⅓ *cup butter*
4 *tablespoons flour*
2½ *quarts beef or chicken broth*
3 *egg yolks*
¼ *teaspoon white pepper*
2 *tablespoons Parmesan cheese, grated*
   Salt

In large kettle cook cauliflower in boiling salted water just until tender. Remove cauliflower; set aside water in which cauliflower was cooked. Stir butter and flour together in kettle. Add broth and 1 cup cauliflower water. Stir until blended. Heat to boiling and boil 5 minutes. Beat egg yolks with 1 tablespoon cold water; mix with a small amount of the broth, then add to kettle. Bring to a boil. Add cauliflower, cheese, pepper, and salt to taste. Serve at once. Serves 6.

CAULIFLOWER-VEGETABLE SAUTÉ

1 *medium head cauliflower, separated into flowerets*
6 *small zucchini, cut in ½-inch slices*
1 *green pepper, cut in strips*
2 *tablespoons onion, chopped*
4 *tablespoons butter*
1 *teaspoon garlic salt*
¼ *teaspoon pepper*
2 *medium tomatoes, cut in wedges*
¼ *cup Parmesan cheese, grated*

In medium skillet sauté cauliflower, zucchini, green pepper, and onion in butter 5 minutes. Add garlic salt and pepper. Cover and simmer 10 to 12 minutes, stirring occasionally. Add tomatoes and cook gently 5 minutes. Sprinkle with Parmesan cheese before serving. Serves 4 to 6.

CELERY

How to Use: Use stalks with leaves for nibblers or garnish.

Stuff stalks with cream cheese, cheese spread, peanut butter, and egg or tuna salad for snacks.

Chop or slice and add to tossed salads, or vegetable or meat salads.

Mince and add to ground meat, onion, and mayonnaise for sandwich spreads.

Add chopped celery to carrots, green beans, peas, or tomatoes while cooking.

Cook chunks of celery in broth. Season to taste with basil, thyme, or tarragon.

CORN

WHOLE KERNEL CORN

How to Use: Confetti salad: Mix corn with diced celery, chopped tomato, salt, pepper, and French dressing. Chill. Serve on lettuce leaves.

Add cooked corn to scrambled eggs. Add sautéed onions, if desired. Season to taste with salt, pepper, and cumin.

Add to green peppers sautéed in butter. Cook until lightly browned.

Mexican corn: Sauté diced green peppers in butter. Add corn, pimiento, and chopped onion; sauté 5 minutes, stirring frequently.

Bacon-Corn Sauté: Fry bacon until crisp; break into bits. Drain off most of bacon drippings. Sauté cooked or uncooked corn in bacon fat 5 minutes, stirring constantly. Add bacon bits before serving.

Use in Succotash.

Use for corn relish, or in scalloped corn.

Add corn kernels to muffin batter before baking. If desired, add crumbled cooked bacon and minced green pepper. Bake according to recipe directions.

Corn and Cheese Sauté: Sauté corn in butter along with 1 clove minced garlic, a dash of salt and pepper, and a little light cream. Cover and simmer 15 minutes, stirring occasionally. Remove from heat. Sprinkle with Parmesan cheese; cover pan until cheese melts.

Southern-style Corn: Cook whole-kernel corn in melted butter mixed with flour, sugar, salt, and milk. Cover and cook 10 minutes. Add cream before serving, if desired.

CORN CHOWDER

4 *slices bacon*
1¼ *cups onions, chopped*
4 *medium potatoes, peeled and diced*
½ *cup water*
4 *cups whole-kernel corn*
4 *cups milk*
2 *teaspoons salt*
Pepper to taste
⅛ *teaspoon sugar*

This tastes best when made in advance and reheated. In large saucepan fry bacon until soft. Add onions and continue cooking until bacon is crisp and onions are golden. Add potatoes and water; bring to boil and simmer 10 minutes. Add corn; cook 5 minutes or until vegetables are tender. Add milk, salt, pepper, and sugar. Heat until warmed through. Serves 6.

CREAM-STYLE CORN

How to Use: Add to chowders, vegetable soups, casseroles, and cream soups.

Add to scrambled eggs. If desired, add cooked bacon, fried onion, or diced fried potatoes.

Add to diluted cream of tomato soup. Season with a little sugar, curry powder, salt, and pepper. Heat until warmed through.

CUCUMBERS

How to Use: Cut in thick slices or into sticks; dip in favorite chip dip.

Cucumber Dip: In blender combine 1 cup cottage cheese, 1 or 2 sliced and seeded cucumbers, 2 tablespoons lemon juice, and salt and pepper to taste. Chill several hours. Serve as dip or as topping for baked potatoes.

Dice cucumber and mix with diced tomato, chopped celery, minced onion, and green pepper. Serve in lettuce cups with favorite dressing.

Cucumber Boats: Cut cucumbers lengthwise; scoop out centers, leaving a ⅓-inch shell. Fill with seafood salad, or pickled herring in sour cream combined with chopped radishes, or with diced cucumbers mixed with cottage cheese and lemon juice, and seasoned to taste.

Seafood Garnish: Place a thin slice of unpeeled cucumber on top of a thin lemon slice.

Score edges with a fork; use as garnish for salads, meat or vegetable platters.

Cucumber Relish Salads:

Combine sliced cucumbers, tomatoes, green pepper, onions, salt, pepper, vinegar, sugar, vegetable oil, and a small amount of water. Chill before serving.

Mix sliced cucumbers, sliced onions, and chopped dill with dairy sour cream; chill 1 hour or more before serving.

Toss chopped cucumber with canned pineapple chunks, cooked bacon, and crumbled blue cheese. Serve on lettuce leaves.

Cucumber-Tomato Mayonnaise: Combine 1 cup mayonnaise, ½ cup each diced cucumber and tomato, 1 teaspoon minced onion, and a dash of salt. Serve at once over salad greens or cold meats.

Cucumber Salad Dressing: Add diced cucumber to mayonnaise.

Add to Gazpacho.

Slice paper-thin and float on top of soup for garnish.

Fish Sauce: Peel and seed cucumber. Shred enough to make 1 cup cucumber. Add ½ cup dairy sour cream, ¼ cup mayonnaise, 1 tablespoon chopped parsley, 2 teaspoons minced onion, ¼ teaspoon salt, 1 teaspoon white wine vinegar, and pepper to taste. Chill. Serve with hot or cold fish or seafood.

CHILLED CUCUMBER SOUP

2 cups buttermilk
1 cucumber, peeled and seeded
3 tablespoons parsley, chopped
1½ tablespoons green onion, sliced
½ teaspoon salt
1 to 2 peppercorns

Place all ingredients in blender. Blend on medium speed for 45 seconds. Chill several hours. Stir before serving. Serves 4 or 5.

CUCUMBER MOLDED SALAD

1 (3-ounce) package lime gelatin
1 medium cucumber, peeled, seeded and diced
1 tablespoon minced onion
2 tablespoons tarragon vinegar
Dash each salt, sugar, and pepper
½ cup salad dressing or mayonnaise
1 cup cottage cheese

In medium bowl dissolve gelatin in 1 cup boiling water. In small bowl combine cucumber, onion, vinegar, salt, sugar, and pepper. Blend salad dressing into gelatin mixture, using a spoon or rotary beater. Add cottage cheese and cucumber mixture. Pour into a 4-cup mold. Chill until firm. Serves 6 to 8.

EGGPLANT

How to Use: Cut, salt, and drain off excess moisture before using in recipes that have no thickening. Sprinkle with lemon juice after cutting to prevent discoloration.

Pare and cut into slices or cubes. Dip into crumbs and sauté in vegetable oil or bacon drippings.

Cut into ½-inch slices and place on cookie sheet. Brush with a mixture of melted butter seasoned with garlic salt, thyme, oregano, marjoram, and paprika. Broil until slightly brown. Turn slices, brush with butter, and broil until tender. If desired, top each slice with a slice of cheese and heat until cheese is melted.

Stuffed Eggplant: Cut off top. Scoop out pulp and cook it in water until tender. Combine with mixture of cooked meat and rice or seasoned vegetables with sautéed bacon. Cover with eggplant top. Place in baking pan with a little water in the bottom and bake at 350° until filling is heated through.

GREEN BEANS

How to Use: Marinate cooked beans to serve in salads:

Combine with chopped tomatoes and onions, marinate in Italian dressing and dairy sour cream for several hours. Serve in lettuce cups.

Marinate with cooked wax beans and sliced onion. Serve on lettuce.

Chill in French or Italian dressing; serve on a tomato slice.

Mix with mayonnaise and serve on greens.

Heat cooked beans gently with canned tomatoes and minced onion. Season to taste with salt and pepper.

Ham Boiled Dinner: Add green beans and pared raw potatoes to a picnic ham 30 minutes before meat has finished cooking.

Roman Skillet Green Beans: Mix cooked green beans with equal amount of chopped ripe tomato, a little chopped ham or bacon drippings if desired, and garlic salt and sugar to taste. Heat until warm.

Green Bean Oven Dishes:

Green Bean–Sour Cream bake: Place cooked beans in buttered baking dish. Mix dairy sour cream with garlic salt and pepper; spoon over beans. Top with crumbs. Bake, uncovered, at 350° for 20 minutes.

Baked Green Beans au Gratin: Place cooked green beans in baking dish. Blend condensed cream soup, minced onions, salt and pepper to taste, and shredded cheddar cheese. Thin with milk or bean liquid. Pour sauce over beans. Bake, uncovered, at 350° 30 to 45 minutes.

Green Bean–Tomato Casserole: In greased baking dish layer cooked green beans with chopped tomatoes (fresh or canned), minced onion, salt, oregano, and melted butter, beginning and ending layers with beans. Cover with shredded cheddar cheese, top with crumbs. Bake, uncovered, at 350° 30 minutes.

SWEET-SOUR GREEN BEANS

2 *strips bacon*
1 *cup onion, chopped*
1 *tablespoon flour*
⅔ *cup liquid from vegetables or water*
¼ *cup vinegar*
2 *tablespoons sugar*
1 *teaspoon salt*
¼ *teaspoon pepper*
2 *cups green beans, cooked*

Cook bacon slices. Drain bacon; crumble into bits. Reserve 1 tablespoon bacon drippings. Cook onions in bacon drippings until lightly browned. Stir in flour. Add vegetable liquid or water, vinegar, sugar, salt, and pepper; bring to a boil. Stir in beans; heat until warm. Sprinkle with crumbled bacon before serving. Serves 4.

CREOLE GREEN BEAN BAKE

2 *tablespoons butter or margarine*
1 *medium onion, chopped*
1 *tablespoon flour*
¾ *cup tomato juice*
2 *cups cooked green beans*
½ *cup cheddar cheese, shredded*
1 *green pepper, finely chopped*
¼ *teaspoon salt*
¾ *cup fresh bread crumbs, buttered*

In small skillet sauté onion in butter until tender. Add flour and tomato juice. Stir until thickened; set aside. In separate container combine beans, cheese, green pepper, and salt. Place in a greased 1½-quart baking dish; pour tomato mixture over beans. Sprinkle bread crumbs over top. Bake, uncovered, at 350° 20 minutes. Serves 4 to 6.

GREEN BEANS PARMESAN

2 *tablespoons vegetable oil*
2 *cups cooked green beans*
1 *tablespoon vinegar*
1 *tablespoon vegetable oil*
2 *teaspoons onion, minced*
¼ *teaspoon salt*
½ *cup plain or flavored croutons*
2 *tablespoons grated Parmesan cheese*

In medium skillet heat 2 tablespoons oil and green beans over moderate heat, stirring occasionally. In small container mix vinegar, 1 tablespoon oil, onion, and salt; pour over warmed beans and toss gently. Toss in croutons and sprinkle with Parmesan cheese. Serve immediately. Serves 4.

SWISS BEANS

2 *tablespoons butter or margarine*
2 *cups green beans, cooked*
4 *ounces canned mushrooms, if desired*
¼ *cup onion, chopped*
2 *tablespoons flour*
1 *teaspoon salt*
  Dash marjoram, pepper, and thyme
¾ *cup milk*
½ *to 1 cup Swiss cheese, shredded*

In a medium-size ovenproof skillet melt butter; sauté mushrooms and onions. Stir in flour and seasonings. Gradually stir in milk; heat, stirring frequently, until mixture is thick. Remove from heat. Stir in beans and half the cheese. Sprinkle with remaining cheese. Cover and heat gently until beans are heated through and cheese is melted. Or bake uncovered at 400° until cheese is melted. Serves 4.

DOWN HOME GREEN BEANS

> 2 *slices bacon, cut in sections, cooked and drained (reserve*
> *drippings)*
> 2 *cups uncooked green beans*
> 1 *medium onion, sliced*
> 1 *cup raw or cooked tomatoes*
> ¼ *cup water*
> ½ *teaspoon salt*
> *Dash pepper*
> ⅛ *teaspoon sugar*

In medium saucepan combine beans, onions, tomatoes, water, sugar, salt, and pepper; bring to a boil. Cover and simmer 15 to 20 minutes or until beans are tender. Stir in small amount of bacon drippings and the cooked bacon. Serves 4.

SCANDINAVIAN GREEN BEAN SALAD

> 2 *cups green beans, cooked and drained (reserve 2 tablespoons*
> *liquid)*
> ¼ *cup vinegar*
> 1 *tablespoon vegetable oil*
> 2 *tablespoons sugar*
> 1 *teaspoon dill weed*
> ¼ *teaspoon ground allspice*
> ¼ *teaspoon salt*
> *Dash pepper*
> ¼ *cup pickled cocktail onions*
> ¼ *cup radishes, thinly sliced*
> *Canned tuna or salmon*

In medium bowl with cover combine vinegar, oil, spices, and 2 tablespoons bean liquid. Add beans and toss gently. Cover and chill at least 1 hour. At serving time add onions and radishes; toss lightly. Serve with salmon or tuna. If desired, garnish with hard-cooked or deviled eggs. Spoon extra sauce over fish. Serves 4.

GREEN ONIONS

How to Use: Mix with cooked peas for salad.
 Sprinkle thin slices of onion on soups for garnish.
 Add to fried rice.

Add to pan juices of broiled or fried meat. Season to taste
with herbs, Worcestershire sauce, butter, and so on. Heat
gently and serve over meat.

Green Onion Quiche: Sauté 3 cups chopped green onions
with tops in butter. Add salt and pepper, 1 cup milk, 1 cup
dairy sour cream, and 2 beaten eggs. Pour into 9-inch unbaked pie shell; bake at 400° 15 minutes, then at 350° for
30 to 40 minutes.

GREEN PEPPER

How to Use: Cut into strips to use for munching and dipping.

Cut into rings and fill with cole slaw or chopped vegetables.

Cut into rings and use for garnish. Combine with onion rings
or red pepper rings for added color.

Sauté and add to scrambled eggs.

Cut into large squares and place on skewers along with meat
and vegetable chunks; cook on outdoor grill.

SAUTÉED VEGETABLE ACCOMPANIMENT

¼ *pound fresh or canned mushrooms, sliced*
6 *green onions with tops, sliced*
1 *green pepper, cut into strips*
3 *tablespoons butter*
Salt to taste

In medium skillet combine vegetables and butter; sauté over moderate heat
until vegetables soften slightly, about 5 minutes. Add small amount of salt.
Serve at once with steak or hamburgers. Makes about 2 cups vegetables.

TOMATO-PEPPER STEAK

2 *pounds round steak, cut in thin strips*
⅓ *cup vegetable oil*
Dash garlic powder
1 *teaspoon salt*
Dash pepper
¼ *teaspoon ground ginger*
¼ *cup soy sauce*
1 *onion, sliced*
1 *green pepper, cut in 1-inch pieces*
6 *tomatoes, quartered*

3 *tablespoons sugar*
2 *(16-ounce) cans bean sprouts or 4 cups fresh bean sprouts*
2 *tablespoons cornstarch*
½ *cup water*
4 *cups hot cooked rice*

In large skillet with cover, brown steak in oil with garlic, salt, pepper, and ginger. Cover and simmer 30 minutes. Add soy sauce, onion, and green pepper. Cover and cook 5 minutes. Add tomatoes and sugar; cook 5 minutes. Stir in bean sprouts. In small bowl blend cornstarch and water. In center of skillet make a well; pour cornstarch mixture into well; stir until thickened, then stir into rest of pan. Cook until thickened, stirring constantly. Serve over rice. Serves 6 to 8.

KOHLRABI

How to Use: Cut in slices and eat raw. If desired, serve with appetizer dip.
Slice thinly and add to tossed salads, vegetable salads, or cole slaw.
Sauté sliced kohlrabi in vegetable oil or bacon drippings.
Peel kohlrabi, dice, and cook in salted water or chicken broth until tender, 15 to 20 minutes. If desired, cook chopped leaves in separate pan until wilted, about 3 minutes. Combine leaves with cooked kohlrabi. Add butter, salt, and pepper to taste. Or drain and place in a seasoned cream sauce or cheese sauce.

LETTUCE

How to Use: Use as part of greens in tossed salads.
Use individual leaves to top a meat, cheese, egg, or meat salad sandwich. Serve open-faced or top with second slice of bread.
Use small leaves to form decorative edging for vegetable or fruit salads.
French Peas and Lettuce: Combine 2 cups fresh or frozen peas, ⅓ cup chopped onion or small whole onions, 6 shredded lettuce leaves, salt and pepper, and a pinch of sugar. Cover tightly and cook until peas are tender. Add a small amount of water, if necessary. Add 2 tablespoons butter, toss, and serve.

Leftover lettuce from a salad: Wash lettuce leaves. Combine with broth, seasonings and cooked vegetables; puree in blender. Serve hot or cold as a soup. Or chop lettuce finely and add to cream soups.

OKRA

How to Use: Use in chicken or beef gumbo.

Steam whole or cut okra until tender, 5 to 8 minutes. Serve with butter, Hollandaise sauce, or mayonnaise.

Slice and coat with corn meal; fry in bacon drippings or vegetable oil.

Sauté okra with desired combinations of celery, onion, or green peppers. If desired, add diced tomatoes or green onions.

Marinate cooked okra in French dressing. Serve chilled over lettuce leaves.

PARSLEY

How to Use: Store fresh parsley upright, stem side down, in tall, tightly covered jar.

Add to tossed salads, vegetable salads, and aspics.

Use for garnish: Use sprigs alone or chop finely and sprinkle over foods. Slip a parsley sprig into a cross section of carrot with its center core removed. Mince parsley and use to coat a lemon section for a seafood garnish.

Use in soups, stews, casseroles, and skillet dinners for color appeal.

Chop and sprinkle over cooked vegetables.

Chop and add to sandwich spreads.

To freeze parsley, chop and place 2-tablespoon portions in ice cube compartments of an ice cube tray. Fill tray with water and freeze. Thaw as needed.

PARSNIPS

How to Use: Shred and add raw parsnips to vegetable salads or tossed salads.

Pare and cut into halves, quarters or slices. Remove center core if tough. Steam until tender. Serve with melted butter.

Cut into sections and add to pot roast along with potatoes, carrots, celery, turnips, and onions. Cook until vegetables are tender, about 45 minutes.

Pare, slice, and sauté in butter until tender.

Bake pared sliced parsnips at 350° 30 to 45 minutes. Before baking dot with butter and season with salt. Add water or broth to cover bottom of baking dish. Cover and bake.

Add quartered pared parsnips to browned seasoned pork chops. Add water; cover and simmer until chops and parsnips are tender. Thicken liquid with a flour-water paste to make gravy.

PEAS, COOKED GREEN

How to Use: Add to chef salads, tossed vegetable salads, aspics, and molded vegetable salads.

Add to soups for color.

Pea-cheese Salad: Combine cubes of cheese, drained cooked peas, chopped celery, minced onion, salt and pepper to taste, and mayonnaise or salad dressing. Chill before serving.

Peas and Bacon Salad: Combine drained cooked peas with cooked bacon and chopped green onions. Moisten with dairy sour cream or mayonnaise. Season to taste with salt and pepper. Chill before serving. Mound mixture on lettuce leaf; garnish with tomato quarters, if desired.

Green and White Salad: Add cooked peas, chopped green onion, and sliced celery to salad greens. Toss with mayonnaise or clear French dressing.

Mix with cooked rice. Serve hot as vegetable; or chill, moisten with French dressing, and serve as salad.

Add to seafood-macaroni salads along with celery, onion, salt and pepper, and mayonnaise or salad dressing.

Add to other cooked vegetables such as carrots, corn, or green beans.

Combine with cooked small onions. Heat gently before serving.

Add to creamed potatoes, scrambled eggs, or soufflés.

Add to cream sauces to serve over meat loaf, fish loaf, croquettes, or hash.

PEAS, EDIBLE POD (SNOW PEAS)

How to Use: Steam until tender. Serve hot or chill and marinate with French dressing and serve on lettuce.

Cook with thin sticks of carrots.

Simmer in milk until tender.

Add to vegetable stews.

Stir-fry with chopped raw pork and water chestnuts. Add chicken broth and steam until tender. Season with salt or soy sauce. Thicken with a cornstarch-water mixture. Serve over rice.

Stir-fry with green onion tops and sliced celery. Add a combination of 1 tablespoon cornstarch, ½ teaspoon salt, 1 teaspoon sugar, 1 tablespoon soy sauce, and ½ cup water; cook, stirring constantly, until peas are barely tender.

Add to pot roast or Swiss steak about 8 minutes before meat has finished cooking.

Polynesian Chicken Almond: Sauté diced cooked chicken 10 minutes. Add sliced celery, mushrooms, bamboo shoots, water chestnuts, and peas; sauté 5 minutes. Add enough chicken broth to cover. Thicken with cornstarch-water mixture. Add salt to taste; simmer 5 minutes. Serve over chow mein noodles. Garnish with blanched whole toasted almonds.

POTATOES

POTATOES, BOILED OR STEAMED

How to Use: Add to soups, chowders, and stews.

Use in favorite hash recipe.

Use in potato salad.

Cube and add to bacon fried with chopped onion. Drain bacon drippings to amount desired. Cook until potatoes are slightly browned. Add beaten eggs, salt and pepper to taste; cook until eggs are set, stirring frequently. Use up to 1½ cups potatoes for every 4 eggs.

Use-It-Up Hash: Combine diced cooked meat or cheese with cooked chopped vegetables. Add an equal amount of diced cooked potatoes. Mix well. Moisten with catsup, cream, bouillon, or broth. Season to taste. Fry in a well-greased covered skillet over high heat until brown on one side. Turn out onto serving platter.

Potatoes and Peas: Combine cubed cooked potatoes with cooked peas. Add melted butter, cooked bacon, and lemon juice.

Slice and fry in vegetable oil until golden brown. If desired, roll in crumbs or seasoned flour before frying.

Slice, roll in seasoned flour, and place in baking pan. Dribble with melted shortening and bake in hot oven until browned.

Potatoes au Gratin: Prepare a cheese sauce flavored with salt, pepper, and a small amount of prepared mustard or minced onion. Place diced cooked potatoes in greased baking dish; cover with cheese sauce. Top with grated cheese if desired. Bake at 350° 20 minutes or until warmed through.

French Potato Salad: Marinate cubed cooked potatoes and equal amounts of canned seafood (tuna, salmon, or shrimp) in clear French dressing, each in a separate bowl, at least 1 hour. At serving time combine potatoes and seafood; add a small amount of chopped pickle and enough mayonnaise to moisten. Serve on lettuce with tomato slices, hard-cooked egg slices, parsley, and ripe olives.

SCALLOPED COOKED POTATOES

4 *cups cooked potatoes, sliced or diced*
· 2 *cups white sauce or 1 (10-ounce) can cream soup plus ⅓*
soup can of milk
Grated cheese or crumbs for garnish, if desired

In 1½-quart greased baking dish place potatoes; cover with white sauce. Bake, uncovered, at 350° for 45 minutes. Top with cheese or crumbs during last 15 minutes, if desired.

CONTINENTAL POTATO SALAD

2 *cups green beans, cooked*
4 *cups cooked potatoes, diced*
2 *tablespoons green onions, sliced*
Up to 1½ cups cooked peas or asparagus tips, if desired
⅔ *cup French or Italian dressing*
⅔ *cup mayonnaise*
¼ *teaspoon salt*
Lettuce cups
Sliced ripe olives or chopped parsley for garnish, if desired

Combine potatoes, onions, green beans, and desired vegetables. Add French or Italian dressing; toss lightly. Cover and chill several hours, stirring occasionally. Drain off dressing, reserving 2 tablespoons. Combine reserved dressing with mayonnaise and salt. Add to potato-vegetable mixture and toss. Serve on lettuce with desired garnish. Serves 8.

POTATOES IN SOUR CREAM

> 4 *medium potatoes, cooked and diced*
> ¼ *cup butter*
> *Salt and pepper to taste*
> 2 *tablespoons minced parsley*
> ½ *cup dairy sour cream*
> 2 *slices bacon, cooked and crumbled*

In medium skillet melt butter. Add potatoes, salt and pepper, and parsley. Cook over moderate heat, stirring frequently, until heated through. Remove from heat. Stir in sour cream. Sprinkle with bacon before serving. Serves 4.

POTATOES, MASHED

How to Use: Steam-heat and serve with hot turkey or beef sandwiches.

Add to stews to help thicken them.

Combine with cooked mashed carrots or rutabagas. Add grated apple if desired. Heat and season to taste.

Mound over cooked meat and vegetables in gravy. Bake in hot oven until potatoes are lightly browned.

Combine with flaked fish or minced cooked chicken; season and shape into patties and fry in vegetable oil until browned. Turn and fry other side.

Mashed Potato Dumplings: Combine 1 cup mashed potatoes with 1 teaspoon salt. Beat in 2 eggs. Add enough flour to make a stiff dough. Form into 1-inch balls and drop into a pan of boiling salted walter. Cook 10 minutes. Put in a strainer and run under cold water. Serve with stews and roasts, or slice and fry in butter with sliced onions.

Mashed Potato Patties: Mix potatoes with egg or onions, and fry in butter until golden brown. If desired, dip in beaten egg and then into flour before frying.

Mashed Potato Casserole: Combine 2 to 3 cups mashed potatoes, ½ cup dairy sour cream, ½ cup grated sharp cheese, ½ teaspoon seasoned salt, and 4 tablespoons melted butter (optional). Sprinkle with paprika and dot with butter. Bake uncovered at 350° 45 minutes. Serve with roast beef, lamb, or turkey. Mixture can also be mounded over a cooked stew and baked until potatoes are golden. If desired, prepare mixture in advance and refrigerate it for up to 24 hours before baking. Serves 4 to 6.

QUICK POTATO SOUP

1 *small onion, chopped*
2 *tablespoons butter*
1 *tablespoon flour*
1 *teaspoon salt*
  Dash pepper
1 *cup water*
1 *cup mashed potatoes*
2 *cups milk*
½ *cup shredded cheese, if desired*

In medium saucepan cook onion in butter until golden. Blend in flour, salt, pepper, and water. Cook, stirring frequently, for 2 minutes. Add potato, milk, and cheese, if desired. Heat until warmed through and cheese is melted. Serves 4.

POTATOES, BAKED

How to Use: Reheat by dipping in water and rebaking at 350° 20 minutes; or place in pan of hot water, bring to a boil, and remove at once.

Peel, dice, and use as cooked boiled potatoes.

Cube peeled baked potatoes, toss in cream to coat all surfaces, and heat in moderate oven 20 minutes. Add cubes of cheddar cheese and season to taste with salt and pepper Toss mixture and bake until cheese is melted.

POTATOES, FRENCH-FRIED

How to Use: Dice and add to scrambled eggs.

Dice and add to many of the recipes which use boiled potatoes (see "Potatoes, Boiled or Steamed").

RADISHES

How to Use: Slice paper-thin and use for soup garnish.

Make radish roses to use for garnish. Cut off root end and stem end. Cut thin petals from stem to root end. Place in cold water and chill.

Radish Sandwiches: Arrange thinly sliced radishes on buttered bread.

Vegetable Relish: Mix canned pineapple chunks, thinly sliced radishes, shredded carrot, and finely chopped green pepper together. Top with a vinegar and oil dressing. Serve with baked or fried fish or with grilled hamburgers.

RUTABAGAS

How to Use: Use interchangeably with turnips.

Add to stews and boiled dinners.

Combine cooked mashed rutabagas with an equal amount of mashed potatoes.

Mix 1 or 2 cups cooked mashed rutabagas with 1 beaten egg mixed with ½ teaspoon salt. Shape into patties. Roll in flour and sauté in vegetable oil at low temperature. Top with dairy sour cream and chives if desired. Patties may also be made without egg, following the above instructions.

Season mashed cooked rutabagas with chives, green onions, parsley, or nutmeg. Heat gently.

Sprinkle cooked slices of rutabaga with a combination of brown sugar, ginger, salt, and pepper. Cook in butter over low heat until sugar melts.

SPINACH

How to Use: Raw spinach: Wash leaves, tear off veins. Add bite-size pieces of spinach leaves to tossed salads or use as base for spinach salad.

Chop cooked spinach and add to beef or chicken broth for a quick soup.

Chopped cooked spinach may be added to scrambled eggs. Add grated cheese, if desired.

Add 1 cup cooked spinach to a 4-egg soufflé.

Creamed Spinach: Sauté a little minced onion in butter. Add flour and liquid from drained cooked spinach; cook until thickened. Add spinach and heat gently.

Creamed Spinach on Toast: Add chopped cooked spinach to a white sauce. Serve over toast or muffins with bacon and tomato slices.

Spinach-Cheese Casserole: Spread cooked spinach in a greased baking dish. Cover with cooked bacon pieces, canned mushrooms, and a dash of pepper. Bake at 325° until heated. Cover with a thin layer of dairy sour cream and a layer of shredded sharp cheddar cheese. Return to oven and heat until cheese melts. Serve over toast or English muffin.

CREAM OF SPINACH SOUP

1 *tablespoon butter*
1 *tablespoon flour*
½ *teaspoon salt*
¼ *teaspoon dry mustard*
¾ *cup chicken or beef broth*
¾ *cup spinach, chopped*
¼ *cup carrots, shredded*
¼ *cup onion, minced*
½ *to 1 cup milk*

In medium saucepan melt butter; blend in flour, salt, and mustard. Stir in broth. Heat, stirring constantly, to boiling. Add spinach, carrots, and onion; cook over medium heat until vegetables are just tender. Stir in milk and heat to serving temperature. Serves 2 to 3.

SPINACH-HAMBURGER SCRAMBLE

1 *pound ground beef*
2 *tablespoons onion, minced*
1 *cup spinach, cooked and chopped*
4 *eggs, beaten*
Salt and pepper to taste
Grated Parmesan cheese

In medium skillet cook beef and onion until meat is no longer red. Drain excess fat. Add spinach and heat until warmed through. Add eggs, salt, and pepper. Stir over low heat until eggs are set. Sprinkle with cheese and serve at once. Serves 4 to 6.

SUMMER SQUASH

How to Use: Cut in strips to use for dips.

Dice and add to tossed salads.

Substitute for zucchini squash in many recipes.

Steam; season with mayonnaise or dairy sour cream and chopped green onions or herbs of choice.

Simmer squash chunks in white sauce or milk. Season to taste.

Sauté in vegetable oil or bacon drippings; season with basil or thyme, minced onion or garlic, salt, and pepper. Cover and simmer until tender.

Bake squash by cutting into sections, brushing with vegetable oil, and placing in 400° oven 10 to 15 minutes. Season with salt, Parmesan cheese, parsley, or paprika.

Parboil squash chunks. Cover with tomato sauce and Parmesan cheese. Bake in moderate oven until heated through.

Scalloped Summer Squash: Parboil squash 3 minutes; drain. Sauté onions in butter. Add flour and cream or milk to make a thick cream sauce. Season with salt, pepper, and a dash of nutmeg. Pour sauce over squash. Top with buttered crumbs. Bake at 350° for 20 minutes.

SUMMER SQUASH IN A SKILLET

4 *strips bacon*
3 *or 4 summer squash, sliced*
2 *cups cooked tomatoes with liquid*
1 *medium onion, chopped*
Salt and pepper to taste
⅛ *teaspoon sugar*

Cut bacon in 1-inch pieces; sauté bacon and onion in medium skillet. Drain off all but 1 tablespoon of bacon drippings. Add squash, tomatoes, salt and pepper, and sugar. Cover and simmer 15 to 20 minutes or until squash is tender. Serves 6.

SUMMER SQUASH–CHEESE SKILLET

> 3 *or 4 summer squash, sliced*
> 2 *tablespoons vegetable oil*
> 1 *small clove garlic, minced*
> ½ *cup onion, chopped*
> ⅛ *teaspoon basil*
>   *Pepper to taste*
> 1 *teaspoon salt*
> ½ *cup mild cheese, shredded*
> ½ *cup canned or fresh tomatoes, chopped*
>   *Dash salt*
> ¼ *teaspoon sugar*

In medium skillet sauté squash, garlic, onion, basil, and pepper in oil. Cover and simmer 10 minutes or until squash is tender. Add 1 teaspoon salt and the cheese. Stir until cheese melts; place on serving dish. In same skillet, heat tomatoes, salt, and sugar quickly; pour over squash. Serves 4 to 6.

WINTER SQUASH

How to Use: Bake squash halves until tender. Fill with cooked meat and/or vegetables in white sauce or in cream soup. Return to oven until heated through.

Bake until tender. Scoop out squash; fluff and add crisp bacon pieces, chopped toasted walnuts, cheddar-cheese cubes, butter, salt, and pepper. Sprinkle with additional chopped walnuts. Serve immediately.

Leftover cooked squash:

Place in baking dish; cover with applesauce or partially cooked bacon strips; cover and bake until heated and bacon is completely cooked.

Mix squash with chopped green onions, dairy sour cream, salt and pepper to taste. Place in greased baking dish. Cover and bake until heated.

Thin cooked squash with cream or orange juice. If desired, sprinkle with crushed pineapple or raisins. Bake, covered, in moderate oven until heated through.

SQUASH PUFF

3 *cups squash, cooked (reserve cooking liquid)*
½ *teaspoon salt*
¼ *teaspoon onion salt*
⅛ *teaspoon pepper*
1 *teaspoon sugar*
¼ *teaspoon nutmeg*
1 *tablespoon butter, melted*
2 *tablespoons flour*
2 *teaspoons baking powder*
1 *egg, beaten*
¼ *cup dry bread crumbs*

In medium bowl mash squash. Add salt, onion salt, pepper, sugar, nutmeg, and butter; mix well. In a 1-cup measure combine flour and baking powder. Add a small amount of squash cooking liquid; stir to blend, then add enough liquid to make ¾ cup. Add egg. Blend liquid ingredients into squash mixture. Turn into greased 1½-quart casserole; sprinkle with crumbs. Bake, uncovered, at 325° 35 minutes. Serves 6.

TOMATOES

TOMATO JUICE

How to Use: Use as part of broth in homemade soups such as vegetable, bean, chicken gumbo, Manhattan clam chowder, Bouillabaisse, Borscht, Gazpacho.

Use for part of liquid in preparing canned condensed soups such as vegetable, meat-vegetable, or bean.

As part of liquid in making meat loaf or meat balls.

As part of cooking liquid for pot roast, stew, or Swiss steak.

Add to gravy in place of water of vegetable-cooking liquid.

Season to taste and use to baste fish while baking or broiling.

Substitute part tomato juice for cooked tomatoes in many recipes. See "Tomato Products Substitution Chart" and "Canned or Cooked Tomatoes" section.

Use in tomato aspics: Use 1 cup tomato juice to each tablespoon of unflavored gelatin. If desired, add any combination of grated onion, shredded carrots, diced celery, chopped nuts, lemon juice, mayonnaise, cottage cheese, stuffed olives, green pepper, Worcestershire sauce, salt, and pepper.

Tomato Juice Cocktail: Season to taste with chopped celery, parsley, green pepper, lemon juice, onion, garlic, cucumber, sugar, salt, and pepper. Liquefy in blender. Chill before serving.

Tomato Juice Bouillon: Combine tomato juice with equal amounts of chicken or beef broth. Heat and season to taste with Worcestershire, salt, and hot pepper sauce, if desired.

Tomato-Pineapple Juice Cocktail: Use equal amounts of chilled tomato juice and pineapple juice. Pour tomato juice into a clear juice glass. Slowly pour in pineapple juice at one side for a rainbow effect. Serve at once.

INSTANT BORSCHT

2 cups tomato juice
2 cups cooked beets, diced, with ½ cup cooking liquid
1½ cups beef broth
1 tablespoon lemon juice
½ teaspoon onion salt
¼ teaspoon celery salt
Dairy sour cream

In medium saucepan combine all ingredients except sour cream; bring to a boil. Reduce heat and simmer 5 minutes. Whirl in blender until smooth. Serve hot or chilled, topped with a tablespoon of sour cream. Serves 5 or 6.

PORK CHOPS AND RICE

2 tablespoons vegetable oil
4 pork chops
1 cup rice, uncooked
Salt to taste
4 thick onion slices
4 lemon slices
4 tablespoons chili sauce
2 cups tomato juice
Dash Tabasco sauce

In ovenproof skillet brown chops in oil; set aside. Drain off all but 2 tablespoons of oil. Stir in rice to coat with oil. Place chops over the rice and sprinkle with salt. Cover each chop with a slice of onion, a slice of lemon, and 1 tablespoon chili sauce. Combine tomato juice and Tabasco; pour over all. Cover and bake at 325° 1 hour. Serves 4.

CANNED OR COOKED TOMATOES

How to Use: Use to make tomato sauce.

Add up to ¾ cup to 1 pound ground beef for meat loaf.

Heat with sugar, salt, pepper, and butter. Season with a pinch of basil, savory, or oregano. Add fresh or cooked corn if desired. Heat 10 minutes.

Add to cooked green beans. Include minced onion, if desired. Heat gently. Season to taste.

Bake with fresh seasoned vegetables. Add a small amount of raw rice if desired. Bake in tightly covered container at 350° for 1 hour or cook on stove top for 30 minutes.

See "Tomato Products Substitution Chart," page 104.

SPICY TOMATO SAUCE

2 *tablespoons butter or margarine*
1½ *tablespoons onion, minced*
1 *small clove garlic, minced*
2 *cups cooked tomatoes, pureed*
¼ *bay leaf*
Salt and pepper to taste

In small saucepan melt butter. Add onion and garlic; cook until soft. Add tomatoes, bay leaf, salt, and pepper. Cook 30 minutes, stirring occasionally. Remove bay leaf. Serve over croquettes, fish, hamburgers, and so on. Makes about 2 cups.

GREEN TOMATOES

How to Use: Use for green tomato pickles, green tomato relishes (such as Piccalilli).

Slice, dip in corn meal, and fry.

Use fried green tomatoes as a base for serving omelets. Top with seasoned tomato sauce, if desired.

Add sliced green tomatoes to onion sautéed in butter. Cook until tender. Season with paprika, salt, and curry powder.

Add quartered green tomatoes to a pot roast 30 minutes before roast has finished cooking. Add a chopped onion, one clove minced garlic, salt and pepper to taste, 1 teaspoon each basil and cumin. Cover and simmer 30 minutes. Thicken cooking liquid with flour and water to make gravy. Slice roast and serve over noodles with gravy.

Pork Chop–Green Tomato Casserole: Place layers of onion slices and green tomato slices in greased baking dish, sprinkling each layer with curry powder and salt. Cover with lightly browned, seasoned pork chops. Cover and bake at 350° 1 hour.

FRIED GREEN TOMATOES

4 *medium green tomatoes, sliced ¼-inch thick*
2 *tablespoons vegetable oil or butter*
  Salt and pepper to taste
¼ *teaspoon garlic powder, if desired*
½ *to 1 teaspoon curry powder, if desired*
¼ *cup flour*
1 *teaspoon sugar*
  Chopped fresh parsley
  Lemon wedges

Combine salt, pepper, flour, sugar, curry powder, and garlic powder. Dip tomato slices in the flour mixture. In heated medium skillet sauté tomatoes in hot oil, cooking both sides. Sprinkle with chopped parsley and serve with lemon wedges.

BEEF AND GREEN TOMATO STEW

1 *(1-pound) pot roast, cut in 1½-inch cubes*
2 *tablespoons flour*
1 *teaspoon salt*
⅛ *teaspoon pepper*
2 *tablespoons vegetable oil*
1½ *cups water*
¼ *teaspoon paprika*
¼ *teaspoon sugar*
1 *onion, sliced*
6 *green tomatoes, washed, cored, and quartered*
4 *medium carrots, sliced*

Combine flour, salt, and pepper; coat meat. Brown meat in oil slowly in large Dutch oven or skillet with tight-fitting cover. Reduce heat and add 1 cup water. Cover and simmer for 1 hour. Add ½ cup water, paprika, sugar, onion, tomatoes, and carrots. Cover and simmer 45 minutes or until vegetables are tender. Serves 4.

GREEN TOMATO PIE

Pastry for one (9-inch) pie crust
⅓ *cup flour*
1½ *cups sugar*
4 *cups thin-sliced green tomatoes*
1 *teaspoon salt*
1 *teaspoon cinnamon*
1 *teaspoon nutmeg*
1 *tablespoon butter*
1 *tablespoon vinegar or 3 tablespoons lemon juice plus 1
teaspoon lemon rind*

Topping:
2 *tablespoons flour*
2 *tablespoons butter*
2 *tablespoons sugar*

In medium bowl combine flour, sugar, tomatoes, salt, cinnamon, nutmeg, and vinegar or lemon juice. Pour into pie shell. Dot with 1 tablespoon butter. Combine topping ingredients and sprinkle over top of pie. Bake 10 minutes in a preheated 400° oven. Reduce heat to 350° and bake 35 to 50 minutes.

RIPE TOMATOES

How to Use: Cut into chunks and use as appetizer with dips made of Roquefort or cream cheese, or dairy sour cream with chives.

Cut into chunks and add to tossed salads.

Use sliced tomatoes in sandwiches along with sliced meat.

Use as a garnish for salads, sandwiches, and main dishes.

Use in spaghetti, chili, or Creole sauces.

Cook and substitute for canned tomatoes. See the "Canned or Cooked Tomatoes" section and "Tomato Products Substitution Chart."

Freeze for later use in cooked dishes. Wash, core, and peel. Steam until tender. Put into freezer bags or containers, leaving ½- to 1-inch head space.

Tomato-Onion Relish: Layer slices of tomato and thin slices of onion in a bowl. Sprinkle each layer with vinegar, salt, and pepper. Cover and chill before using. Keeps several days in refrigerator.

Tomato Salad Platter: Slice tomatoes and place on serving plate. Cover with desired combination of sliced green onions, cooked asparagus tips, avocado slices, cucumber slices, carrot strips, cauliflower flowerets, and so on. Sprinkle with salt and chopped parsley. Pour French dressing over all. Chill 1 hour before serving.

Salad-stuffed Tomatoes: Core uncooked tomatoes and stuff with potato salad, shrimp, chicken or tuna salad, or cottage cheese, corn relish, or vegetable salad.

Place slices of tomato over fish fillets before baking.

Use in Welsh Rarebit.

Baked Stuffed Tomatoes: Wash tomatoes, core, and scoop out seeds and pulp. Season and fill with hash, macaroni and cheese, or sautéed or creamed vegetables. Place in greased baking dish and bake at 375° 30 minutes.

Fried Tomatoes: Slice firm tomatoes. Sprinkle with sugar, if desired, and let stand a few minutes. Coat tomatoes with flour, salt, and pepper; or dip them into a slightly beaten egg and then into fine cracker crumbs. Heat butter or margarine in a skillet; brown tomato slices slowly on both sides. Serve at once, garnished with parsley. If desired, add light cream to the skillet after removing tomatoes; heat and stir to blend in pan drippings. Pour cream over tomatoes.

TOMATO-BACON SALAD

4 to 6 medium or large tomatoes at room temperature
Salt and pepper to taste
1 small onion, sliced in rings
2 tablespoons vinegar
1 teaspoon sugar
6 slices bacon, cut into 1-inch pieces, fried and drained
(reserve drippings)

Peel and quarter tomatoes; sprinkle with salt and pepper. Place tomatoes in dish; cover with onion rings. In small bowl combine vinegar and sugar; stir until sugar is dissolved. Add bacon and as much bacon drippings as desired; pour mixture over tomatoes. Toss gently and serve immediately. Serves 6.

CUCUMBER-TOMATO SALAD

½ *cucumber, scored with fork and sliced*
2 *large tomatoes, peeled and sliced*
2 *tablespoons green peppers, chopped*
½ *teaspoon salt*
¼ *teaspoon pepper*
¼ *teaspoon sugar*
1 *tablespoon onion, minced*
  Pinch basil

Dressing:
1 *tablespoon vinegar*
2 *tablespoons vegetable oil*

Place tomatoes and cucumbers in serving dish; sprinkle with green peppers. Chill. Combine dressing ingredients and chill. Just before serving pour dressing over vegetables. Serves 4.

MEDITERRANEAN TOMATO SALAD

3 *tomatoes, diced or sliced*
1 *medium onion, sliced*
2 *tablespoons vegetable oil*
1 *teaspoon garlic salt*
1 *teaspoon or less oregano*

Combine all ingredients in a small bowl. Chill at least 1 hour before serving. Serves 4.

SPANISH SAUCE FOR OMELET

1 *onion, sliced in thin strips*
¼ *cup canned mushrooms*
2 *tablespoons butter*
1 *green pepper, cut in strips*
1 *tomato, peeled and diced*
  Salt and pepper to taste
  Worcestershire sauce
  Tabasco sauce

In medium skillet, sauté onion in butter 3 minutes. Add green pepper and mushrooms; continue cooking until onion is transparent. Add tomato. Season to taste with salt, pepper, Worcestershire, and Tabasco. Simmer 10 minutes. Serves 2 or 3.

QUICK TOMATO SAUCE

> 2 *medium tomatoes, peeled and cut in chunks*
> ½ *teaspoon sugar*
> 2 *tablespoons butter*
> 2 *tablespoons onion, chopped*
> 1 *clove garlic, minced*
> 4 *tablespoons dry sherry or red wine*
>   *Salt and pepper*
> 1 *tablespoon parsley, chopped*

Sprinkle tomatoes with sugar; set aside. In medium skillet sauté onion and garlic in butter until tender. Add wine. Cook and stir until liquid is slightly reduced. Add tomatoes and heat through. Add parsley. Season to taste with salt and pepper. Serve over steaks or hamburgers. Makes about 1¼ cups sauce.

GARDEN SPAGHETTI SAUCE

> 1½ *cups onion, chopped*
> 3 *pounds ground beef*
> 3 *cloves garlic, minced*
> 18 *peeled ripe tomatoes*
> 2 *or more cups chopped mixed vegetables (celery, green*
>   *pepper, zucchini, carrots)*
> 1 *tablespoon salt*
> 1 *tablespoon sugar*
> 1 *teaspoon or less cayenne pepper*
> 2 *tablespoons chili powder*
> 2 *bay leaves*
> 4 *(12-ounce) cans tomato paste*

Brown onions, ground beef, and garlic in large pan until meat is no longer red. Drain off excess fat. Add remaining ingredients. Cover and cook 2 to 4 hours, stirring occasionally, until sauce is of desired consistency. Pour into freezer containers, leaving 1 inch head space, and freeze. Makes about 3 quarts.

TOMATO PRODUCTS SUBSTITUTION CHART

Recipe calls for:	Use instead:
1 *(8-ounce) can tomato sauce*	3 *large fresh tomatoes, cooked*
1 *cup tomato puree*	1 *cup cooked tomatoes, pureed in blender*
1 *(1-pound) can whole tomatoes*	6 *large tomatoes cooked in ½ cup water or tomato juice*
1 *(1-pound) can stewed tomatoes*	6 *large tomatoes cooked in ½ cup water with onions, green pepper, salt, pepper, and sugar*
6 *ounces tomato paste*	6 *large tomatoes, cooked, and omit 1 cup water from recipe*
Tomato juice	*Use equal parts cooked pureed tomatoes and water*
1 *(10¾-ounce) can tomato soup*	3 *large tomatoes cooked in ½ cup water or tomato juice, pureed*

TOMATO PASTE

How to Use: Tightly cover unused tomato paste remaining in can. Store in freezer until needed. Thaw 1 hour before using or place can in hot water for 15 minutes.

Add small amounts of tomato paste to beef gravy, stew, Swiss steak, pot roast, chili, vegetable soup.

Add up to ⅓ cup tomato paste to gravy used in making hash.

Salad dressing: Mix with mayonnaise or dairy sour cream. Season to taste as desired with lemon juice, salt, pepper, onion or garlic salt, basil or dill weed, pickle relish, or sugar. Thin with milk, if needed. Chill before using.

Seafood Cocktail Sauce: Combine 4 tablespoons tomato paste, ⅓ cup water, ¼ teaspoon Worcestershire, 1 tablespoon pickle relish, 1 teaspoon lemon juice, ½ teaspoon horseradish, dash each of salt, sugar, and pepper. Chill before serving. Makes ½ cup sauce.

Substitute for tomato sauce in cooked dishes by thinning tomato paste with equal parts of water.

Use in Moussaka or spaghetti sauce.

Sauce for pork chops: Mix tomato paste with an equal amount of dry white wine. Add chopped green pepper and sliced mushrooms, if desired. Pour over browned, seasoned pork chops. Cover and simmer until chops are tender.

Gourmet Hamburger Topping: In same skillet in which

hamburgers were fried, mix 1 tablespoon drippings from hamburgers and 2 tablespoons minced onion; sauté briefly. Add ¼ cup red or white wine; bring to rapid boil, stirring constantly to loosen meat drippings. Add ½ cup light cream or milk and 1 tablespoon tomato paste; boil rapidly until slightly thickened. Stir in 2 tablespoons minced parsley. Serve over hamburgers.

CANNED TOMATO SAUCE

How to Use: Add up to ⅓ cup tomato sauce to 1 pound ground beef when making meat loaf.

Use in Swiss steak.

Add to pot roasts and stews in addition to cooking water.

Use in Spanish rice, Jambalaya, Creole dishes, barbecue sauces, spaghetti sauces, tamales, porcupine balls, lasagna, Ratatouille, or Moussaka.

Add up to ½ cup to beef gravy, vegetable soups, chili, baked beans, or pizza sauce.

Season to taste, heat, and pour over browned chicken, chops, or hamburger patties. Cover and simmer until meat is tender. If desired, add dairy sour cream to sauce just before serving.

Salad dressing: Combine ⅓ cup tomato sauce, ⅓ cup vegetable oil, ¼ cup vinegar, 1 teaspoon salt, dash pepper, ¼ teaspoon oregano, ¼ teaspoon soy sauce, and ½ teaspoon dry mustard. Chill before using. Makes about ⅔ cup dressing.

Poor Boy Pizza: Place slice of white bread or English muffin under broiler and toast one side. Spread with small amount of tomato sauce. Sprinkle with oregano and garlic powder. Top with slices of mild cheese. Broil until cheese is melted.

TURNIPS

How to Use: Slice raw turnips paper-thin and add to vegetable salads.

Add chunks of cooked or raw turnips to vegetable soup.

Use interchangeably with rutabaga in most recipes.

Heat chunks of cooked turnips with cooked peas and carrots, butter, parsley, minced onion, and lemon juice.

Add to pot roast for boiled dinner about 45 minutes before meat has finished cooking.

Heat cooked turnips and top with thick cream sauce. Garnish
with chopped parsley or chives.

Substitute for potatoes in recipes calling for scalloped
potatoes.

Combine mashed cooked turnips with mashed potatoes and
diced or grated apples. Season to taste. Heat until warm.

Mix cooked mashed turnips with soft bread crumbs, using
about half as much bread as turnips. Season with sugar,
salt, and pepper. Add 1 beaten egg for each cup of turnips.
Mix well. Place in greased baking dish and bake at 350°
for 1 hour or until firm.

MISCELLANEOUS VEGETABLES

How to Use: Marinate cold cooked vegetables in French dressing and add
to a tossed salad.

Mix together chopped raw or cooked vegetables. Moisten
with seasoned dairy sour cream. Chill and serve as a salad.

Add chopped cooked vegetables to aspics or to lemon-,
orange-, or lime-flavored gelatins. Add 2 tablespoons
lemon juice or vinegar, if desired. Cottage cheese or cubes
of cheese may also be added.

Chilled Vegetable Platter: Cover platter with salad greens.
Arrange chilled cooked vegetables, onion rings, and
tomato slices on greens. Cover with choice of bottled
dressing.

Checkerboard Vegetable Salad: Combine such chopped
cooked vegetables as green beans, corn, peas, carrots,
garbanzo or pea beans. Add chopped raw celery, green
onions with tops, green pepper, parsley, pimiento, and so
on. Add pepper to taste. Make a dressing of ⅓ cup
vinegar, ½ cup sugar, ¼ teaspoon salt; heat until sugar
dissolves. Cool slightly and add ¼ cup vegetable oil. Pour
dressing over vegetables; chill several hours before
serving.

Add chopped cooked vegetables to canned or homemade
soups such as vegetable, minestrone, or mulligatawny.

Add to omelets and scrambled eggs shortly before they have
finished cooking.

Add to a tomato sauce to serve over an omelet.

Add cooked chopped vegetables to cream sauces when
making chicken, turkey or ham à la King, or to cream
sauce to serve over meat loaf or croquettes.

Add chopped, cooked, and drained vegetables to lasagna or spaghetti sauce.

Combine with other cooked vegetables and heat gently in butter. Season as desired with onion, garlic, seasoned salt and pepper.

Vegetables and Bacon in Cream Sauce: Reheat chopped cooked vegetables in a thick cream sauce. Add crisp bacon bits before serving.

Cooked Vegetable Casserole: Combine cooked vegetables with cream soup or tomato soup. Add cooked rice if desired. Bake at 350° 30 minutes. Ten minutes before serving remove from oven and top with crumbs or crushed potato or corn chips. Bake 10 minutes.

Vegetable Patties: Mince cooked vegetables. Add up to 1½ cups vegetables to 2 beaten eggs. Stir in ¼ cup flour and season as desired. In hot greased skillet fry patties like pancakes, using 2 tablespoons of the vegetable mixture for each pattie.

Freeze cooked vegetables in a freezer container until enough accumulate to use in desired recipe.

Add chopped cooked vegetables along with chopped raw onions to a pot roast or round steak during the last half-hour of cooking.

Use-It-Up Cream Soup: Puree up to 1½ cups leftover cooked vegetables or meat. Mix with condensed cream soup. Thin with milk or broth if desired. Heat thoroughly. Season to taste. Serve hot.

QUICK CREAM OF VEGETABLE SOUP

2 *tablespoons butter or margarine*
1 *teaspoon onion, minced*
3 *tablespoons flour*
1 *teaspoon salt*
   Dash pepper
1 *cup cooked pureed vegetables (such as carrots, cauliflower, celery, spinach, peas, broccoli, asparagus, summer squash)*
4 *cups milk (part vegetable broth or chicken broth may be used)*

In medium saucepan sauté onion in butter. Blend in flour until mixture is smooth and bubbly. Stir in vegetables. Bring to boil and cook 1 minute, stirring constantly. Remove from heat. Gradually stir in milk. Heat until warmed through. Season with salt and pepper. Serve immediately. Serves 4 to 6.

RUSSIAN SALAD

Any combination of:
Cooked green beans
Cooked beets, drained well
Cooked carrots
Raw celery
Raw cucumber
Raw onion
Cooked peas or
cooked potatoes
Mayonnaise
Sliced cold meat

Garnish:
Sliced hard-cooked eggs
Green or ripe olives
Tomato quarters
Salad greens

Chop vegetables into ¼-inch cubes. If time allows marinate 1 hour in French dressing. Drain, then toss in mayonnaise. Arrange salad greens on serving plate. Mound salad on greens. Surround with sliced cold meat and garnishes.

VEGETABLE STEW

Any combination of the following raw vegetables: carrots, green or red bell pepper, onion, garlic, green beans, tomatoes, cauliflower, potatoes, eggplant, celery, parsley, zucchini, or yellow summer squash. Slice or chop vegetables. In greased baking dish, layer all vegetables except zucchini and summer squash. Pour 1 cup tomato sauce or canned tomatoes over vegetables. Stir in 1 teaspoon basil and salt to taste. Cover and bake at 350° 45 minutes. Or cover and simmer on stove top 1 hour. Add zucchini and summer squash during last 15 minutes of cooking.

HAMBURGER-STUFFED VEGETABLES

1 pound ground beef
1 cup rice, cooked
½ cup onion, chopped

¼ cup fresh parsley, chopped
1 teaspoon garlic salt
6 large vegetables for stuffing (tomatoes, green peppers,
   zucchini, summer squash, eggplant)
2 cups tomato juice, or 3 cups mixed sliced vegetables such as
   onions, green pepper, mushrooms, tomatoes, summer
   squash, or zucchini

In medium skillet sauté meat until redness disappears; drain off excess fat. Add rice, onion, parsley, and garlic salt. To prepare vegetables for stuffing, cut off tops of tomatoes or green pepper and scoop out pulp and seeds; slice squash lengthwise and scoop out pulp, leaving ½-inch shell. Fill centers of vegetables with meat-rice filling. Grease a large baking dish. Place tomato juice or the mixed sliced vegetables on the bottom of the dish. Cover with stuffed vegetables. Cover dish tightly and bake at 350° for 45 to 50 minutes. Serves 6.

GARDEN CHICKEN

1 large broiler-fryer chicken, cut up
2 tablespoons vegetable oil
1 cup onion, chopped
1 clove garlic, minced
1¼ cups chicken broth
1 teaspoon salt
   Dash Tabasco sauce
½ teaspoon thyme
1 cup diced cooked ham or pork, optional
1 cup carrots, sliced
2 cups green beans, cut
3 small zucchini, sliced
3 tomatoes, peeled and diced
   Cooked rice or noodles

In large skillet sauté chicken pieces in oil until golden brown. Drain and set aside. Cook onion and garlic in chicken drippings until golden. Add broth, salt, Tabasco, thyme, diced ham, and browned chicken. Cover and simmer 40 minutes. Add carrots and beans; cover and cook 15 minutes or until vegetables and chicken are tender. Add zucchini and tomatoes and cook 5 minutes longer. If desired, thicken sauce by adding flour-water paste. Serve over rice or noodles. Serves 6.

USE-IT-UP QUICHE

1 *(9-inch) pie pastry*
½ *to 1 cup thinly sliced or chopped vegetables, raw or cooked*
2 *tablespoons onion, chopped*
1 *clove garlic, minced*
2 *tablespoons vegetable oil*
¾ *teaspoon salt*
¼ *teaspoon pepper*
¼ *teaspoon herbs or seasonings of choice*
3 *eggs, beaten*
½ *cup light cream or evaporated milk*
    Up to ½ cup shredded or grated cheese, if desired
    Up to ½ cup minced cooked meat, poultry or fish, if desired
    Parmesan cheese (optional)

Bake pastry in preheated 450° oven 5 minutes. Sauté vegetables, onion, and garlic in oil 10 to 15 minutes or until tender. Add salt, pepper, and herbs. Spread vegetables over pastry. Combine eggs, cream, cheese, and meat; pour over vegetables. Sprinkle with Parmesan cheese if desired. Bake at 350° 30 minutes or until set. Serves 6.

VEGETABLE-RICE SKILLET

2 *medium zucchini, chopped*
5 *large ripe tomatoes, peeled and chopped*
3 *tablespoons vegetable oil*
½ *cup onion, sliced*
1 *green pepper, cut in strips*
½ *cup raw rice*
    Salt and pepper to taste
4 *tablespoons Parmesan cheese*

In skillet with tight-fitting cover, sauté onion in oil until lightly browned. Add tomatoes, green pepper, zucchini, rice, salt, and pepper. Cover tightly and simmer 35 to 40 minutes, or until rice is tender. Add a little water if mixture gets too dry. Before serving fluff with a fork and sprinkle with Parmesan cheese. Serves 4 to 6.

YAMS

How to Use: Use interchangeably with sweet potatoes in most recipes.
Combine mashed cooked yams with lemon juice, brown sugar, salt, a dash of ground cloves, and butter. Mound over canned peach halves or canned pineapple slices. Place

in buttered baking dish. Top with additional butter. Bake at 400° for 20 minutes.

Mash cooked yams; mix with chopped nuts, softened butter, salt, and a little orange or cranberry juice if desired. Spoon into hollowed-out orange shells. Bake at 350° for 15 minutes. Serve with poultry or game.

Use in place of pastry over a chicken or meat pie or ham casserole. Mix mashed cooked yams with salt, butter, orange juice, and orange rind. Bake at 350° until meat mixture is warmed through and yam topping is lightly browned.

Yam Boats: Scoop out centers of cooked yam halves. Fill with a mixture of the yam pulp, raisins, and cranberry-orange relish. Cover with a mixture of butter, salt, and brown sugar. Top with walnuts. Bake at 350° for 30 minutes.

Yam and Pear Casserole: Combine equal amounts of sliced unpeeled fresh pears and slices of cooked and peeled yams. Arrange in layers in a baking dish; sprinkle pear layers with brown sugar and chopped walnuts. Spread yam layer with generous amounts of butter. Bake at 350° for 45 to 50 minutes.

Cover with orange glaze. To make glaze combine ½ cup granulated sugar, ½ cup brown sugar, ½ cup orange juice, and 1 tablespoon cornstarch in a medium saucepan; cook 5 minutes. Add 4 tablespoons butter. Add salt and pepper to taste. Pour over sliced cooked yams and bake at 325° until hot, basting frequently.

Pineapple Yams: Slice cooked yams. Place in skillet with melted butter. Sprinkle with brown sugar. Place pineapple slices on top of yams. Pour pineapple juice over all. Simmer until heated through.

Meat-Yam Casserole: In greased baking dish combine cooked cubed pork, ham or cooked pork sausage with sliced tart apples. Sprinkle with brown sugar and cinnamon. Moisten with gravy. Cover with cooked sliced or mashed yams. Add salt and pepper to taste. If desired, pour a little cream over the yams. Bake at 350° 30–45 minutes.

ZUCCHINI

How to Use: Peel and slice into strips to use for munching and dipping. Cut in strips or thin slices and add to vegetable salads.

Shred or grate coarsely and add to tossed salads.

Use interchangeably with summer squash in most recipes.

Shred and dice and add to tomato sauces for spaghetti, lasagna, or casseroles.

Use in Ratatouille or Gazpacho.

Grilled Zucchini: Cut zucchini into ¼-inch crosswise slices; place on double thickness of heavy-duty aluminum foil. Add quartered fresh tomatoes, sliced celery, salt, pepper, and a dab of butter. Wrap foil tightly around vegetables. Barbecue over hot coals 15 to 20 minutes, turning once.

Peel, grate, and freeze in 2-cup units for baking.

Zucchini–Cream Cheese Sandwiches: Peel zucchini if desired, cut into thin slices, place on buttered dark bread, and spread with soft cream cheese.

QUICK DILLED ZUCCHINI

2 tablespoons butter
½ cup green onion, chopped
3 cups zucchini, chopped
1 teaspoon lemon juice
½ teaspoon salt
Pepper to taste
½ teaspoon dried dill weed or 1 tablespoon fresh chopped dill weed

In large skillet melt butter. Add onions and cook until tender. Add zucchini, lemon juice, salt, pepper, and dill. Cook over medium heat for 5 minutes, stirring occasionally. Serves 4.

VEGETABLE MEDLEY

¼ cup onion, chopped
1 tablespoon butter
½ cup green beans, cut in 2-inch pieces
2 ears of corn, cut in 1-inch pieces
¼ cup water
½ green pepper, coarsely chopped
3 medium zucchini, sliced
1 large tomato, cut into wedges
Salt and pepper to taste

In medium skillet cook onions in butter until golden. Add beans, corn, and ¼ cup water. Cover tightly and bring to boil; simmer 10 minutes. Add green pepper and zucchini; cook, covered, 5 minutes. Add tomatoes; heat just until warmed. Season to taste. Serves 3 or 4.

ZUCCHINI-TOMATO BAKE

> 4 *medium zucchini, sliced*
> 3 *large tomatoes, sliced*
> 1 *large onion, sliced*
> 1 *teaspoon salt*
> ¼ *teaspoon basil or oregano*
> ⅛ *teaspoon pepper*
> 1 *cup grated Parmesan cheese*
> 3 *tablespoons butter*

In greased 7-by-11-inch baking dish layer zucchini, tomatoes, and onion, sprinkling each layer with salt, basil or oregano, pepper, and cheese. Dot butter over the top layer. Cover tightly and bake at 350° 30 to 40 minutes. Serves 6 to 8.

HAMBURGER-ZUCCHINI SKILLET SUPPER

> 1 *pound ground beef*
> 2 *or 3 medium zucchini*
> 1 *clove garlic, minced*
> 1 *medium onion, chopped*
> *Pinch savory or basil*
> 1 *teaspoon salt*
> *Pepper to taste*
> ½ *cup cheese, diced*
> ¾ *cup canned or fresh tomatoes,*
> *diced*
> ¼ *teaspoon salt*
> ½ *teaspoon sugar*

In large skillet lightly brown ground beef, onion, and garlic; drain off excess fat. Slice zucchini into 1-inch pieces and add to meat mixture. Add savory or basil, and pepper to taste. Cover and simmer 10 to 15 minutes. Add 1 teaspoon salt and the cheese. Stir and place in serving dish. In skillet briefly heat tomatoes, ¼ teaspoon salt, and sugar. Pour over zucchini-meat mixture. Serves 3 or 4.

ROMAN CHOPS

4 *pork or lamb chops*
    (may use pork steak also)
2 *tablespoons vegetable oil*
1 *(8-ounce) can tomato sauce*
1 *clove garlic, minced*
½ *teaspoon basil*
½ *teaspoon oregano*
1 *teaspoon salt*
¼ *teaspoon pepper*
1 *cup tomato, diced*
2 *cups zucchini, sliced*

Trim excess fat from meat. In large skillet brown meat in oil. Add tomato sauce, garlic, basil, oregano, salt, pepper, and diced tomato; stir to blend well. Cover and simmer 20 to 25 minutes. Add zucchini and continue cooking until zucchini is barely tender. Serves 4.

SCALLOPED ZUCCHINI

6 *to 8 medium zucchini, sliced and parboiled*
1 *(1-pound) can cream-style corn*
4 *eggs, beaten*
1 *medium onion, chopped*
1 *green pepper, chopped*
2 *tablespoons butter or vegetable oil*
1 *teaspoon salt*
  Dash pepper
1 *cup cheddar cheese, shredded*
¼ *teaspoon paprika*

In ovenproof 2-quart skillet sauté onion and green pepper in butter until golden. In separate bowl combine zucchini, corn, eggs, salt, and pepper; pour into skillet. Sprinkle with cheese and paprika. Bake, uncovered, at 350° for 40 minutes. Serves 6.

ITALIAN ZUCCHINI CASSEROLE

4 *medium zucchini, sliced and parboiled*
1 *pound ground beef*
1 *medium onion, chopped*
1 *small clove garlic, minced*
½ *teaspoon salt*
½ *teaspoon basil*
¼ *teaspoon oregano*

¼ teaspoon pepper
1 cup rice, cooked
½ cup tomato sauce
½ cup grated mild cheese

In medium skillet sauté ground beef, onion, garlic, and seasonings until onions are transparent; drain off excess fat. Stir in rice and tomato sauce. In greased 1½-quart baking dish arrange half the zucchini slices. Cover with meat-rice mixture, remaining zucchini, and top with grated cheese. Bake uncovered at 350° 25 to 30 minutes or until heated through. Serves 4.

STUFFED ZUCCHINI AS-YOU-LIKE-IT

6 medium zucchini or 6 3-inch slices
    of large zucchini, parboiled
½ to 1 pound ground beef or ground
    lamb; or up to 2 cups cooked beef
    or lamb, minced
1 large clove garlic, minced
½ cup onion, chopped
    If desired, up to 1½ cups cooked rice plus gravy or white
        sauce to moisten
¼ to ½ teaspoon oregano
1 teaspoon salt

Sauce I:
2 tablespoons butter
2 tablespoons flour
1 cup light cream or evaporated milk
¼ teaspoon nutmeg
½ cup Swiss cheese, shredded

Sauce II:
2 cups canned or freshly cooked tomato sauce seasoned with
    oregano

Sauce III:
1 (10½-ounce) can condensed cream soup plus ½ soup can of
    milk

Drain parboiled zucchini; scoop out a hollow, leaving about ½-inch shell; reserve zucchini pulp. In large skillet sauté meat, garlic, onion, oregano, and salt. Drain excess fat. Add zucchini pulp; simmer for 20 minutes, stirring occasionally. If using rice, combine with meat and enough gravy or white sauce to make of desired consistency. Mound mixture into zucchini hollows. Place stuffed zucchini in a greased baking dish; pour in enough water to cover bottom of dish ⅛ inch deep. Any extra stuffing may be shaped into balls and placed beside zucchini in pan. If using Sauce I, melt butter in medium saucepan. Stir in flour and cook until mixture is smooth. Add cream and nutmeg; stir and cook until mixture thickens; pour over zucchini. Bake at 350° 20 minutes. Sprinkle with cheese and bake 5 minutes more or until cheese is melted. If using Sauce II or III, pour over zucchini and bake 25 to 30 minutes. Serves 4 to 6.

ZUCCHINI BREAD AS-YOU-LIKE-IT

3 eggs
1 cup vegetable oil
2 cups sugar (may use part brown sugar if desired)
2 cups zucchini, peeled and grated
1 teaspoon to 1 tablespoon vanilla
3 cups flour
1 teaspoon to 1 tablespoon cinnamon
    (or use any desired combination of ginger, allspice, and
        cloves with cinnamon)
1 teaspoon salt
¼ to 1 teaspoon baking powder, depending on lightness desired
1 teaspoon baking soda
    If desired, up to ¾ cup chopped nuts, raisins, dates, or
        grated coconut; or grated orange or lemon rind to taste

In large bowl beat eggs until light and fluffy. Add oil, sugar, zucchini, and vanilla; mix well. Sift flour, cinnamon and spices, salt, baking powder, and baking soda; add to zucchini mixture and beat until thoroughly blended. Stir in nuts or other additions, if desired. Place in 3 greased and floured loaf pans. Bake at 325° 1 hour. Cool 5 to 10 minutes. Turn out and place on wire racks until completely cool.

ZUCCHINI MUFFINS

Follow above recipe. Pour into muffin tins. Bake at 375° 20 minutes.

QUICK ZUCCHINI CRISP

5 cups zucchini, peeled and chopped
⅓ cup sugar
1 teaspoon cinnamon
¼ cup lemon juice

¾ cup water
⅓ cup butter or margarine
1 cup flour
½ cup brown sugar
½ teaspoon salt
1 teaspoon baking powder

In medium saucepan combine zucchini, sugar, cinnamon, lemon juice, and water. Bring to a boil; reduce heat and simmer 10 minutes. Pour mixture into a greased 7-by-11-inch baking pan. In small bowl mix together butter, flour, brown sugar, salt, and baking powder until crumbly. Sprinkle mixture over zucchini. Bake at 350° 45 minutes. Serve warm or cool, topped with whipped cream, ice cream, or light cream. Serves 6 to 8.

ZUCCHINI BARS

4 eggs, slightly beaten
2 cups zucchini, peeled and grated
1 cup vegetable oil
2 cups sugar
2½ cups flour
½ teaspoon baking powder
½ teaspoon salt
2 teaspoons cinnamon
½ teaspoon baking soda
1 teaspoon vanilla
½ cup chopped nuts
½ cup raisins, if desired

Frosting:
¼ cup butter, softened
1 (3-ounce) package cream cheese, softened
1 tablespoon milk or cream
1 teaspoon vanilla
2 cups powdered sugar

In large bowl combine eggs, zucchini, oil, sugar, flour, baking powder, salt, cinnamon, soda, and vanilla; stir well. Add nuts and raisins, if desired. Pour into a greased 9-by-13-inch pan. Bake at 350° 30 to 35 minutes. Cool before frosting. To make frosting, cream butter and cream cheese together. Stir in milk and vanilla. Blend in powdered sugar and stir until smooth. Spread on top of cooled bars. Store bars in a cool place.

Fruit

APPLE JUICE

How to Use: Mix with other ingredients in blender to use as beverage. Possible combinations are apple juice with ice cream, fruit, eggs, and vegetables.

Apple-Banana Drink: Mix ½ cup unflavored yogurt, ½ cup apple juice, 1 banana, and cinnamon to taste.

Apple-Date Drink: Mix ½ cup apple juice, 1 egg, 2 pitted dates, and ½ apple.

Apple-Cranberry Cooler: Blend apple juice, raw cranberries, an orange, and honey to taste. Strain before serving, if desired.

Use in hot spiced punches.

Heat and add to fruit-flavored or unflavored gelatins in place of water.

Use as part of liquid when preparing cakes, muffins, puddings, or gingerbread.

Use in place of water when preparing cooked prunes or fruit soup.

Pancake syrup: Simmer 1 cup apple juice with 1 stick cinnamon and a few whole cloves 10 minutes. Add ½ cup sugar and 2 tablespoons corn syrup; boil 5 minutes.

Use 2 to 4 cups apple juice for stewing beef or pork. Season with onions, bay leaf, salt, and pepper.

MULLED APPLE JUICE

1 quart apple juice
1 teaspoon whole allspice
1 teaspoon whole cloves
2 sticks cinnamon

In medium saucepan combine all ingredients; cover and simmer for 20 minutes. Remove spices or strain before serving. Serves 6.

WASSAIL

> 1 *cup sugar*
> 2 *cups water*
> 6 *whole cloves*
> 2 *sticks cinnamon*
> 1 *tablespoon chopped candied ginger*
> 2 *whole allspice*
> 1½ *cups orange juice*
> 1 *cup lemon juice*
> 1 *quart apple juice*

In large saucepan, combine sugar and water; boil 10 minutes. Add spices; let stand 1 hour at room temperature. Add juices; bring to a boil. Strain before serving. Makes about 1½ quarts.

APPLES

How to Use: Slice in thin wedges, combine with a thin slice of cheese, and eat for a snack or dessert.

Cut into quarters and spread with peanut butter for a quick snack.

Add to fruit cups.

Use to make applesauce, Apple Brown Betty, apple pie, apple crisp.

Sauté apple slices in bacon or sausage drippings; sprinkle with sugar. Serve with bacon or sausage as a breakfast side dish.

Add apple wedges to sauerkraut before baking.

Core and stuff with sausage or a combination of sausage and sauerkraut. Bake at 375° in a pan with 1 inch of water in the bottom until tender.

Skillet Apple Wedges: Peel and slice apples; sprinkle with lemon juice and sugar. Sauté apples in butter in large skillet, turning once. If desired, cover and simmer until tender. Serve with pork, ham, or chicken, or use to fill baked squash halves.

Apple-Ham Lunch: Place slices of apples over a slice of ham; top with Swiss cheese and broil.

Apple Salads:

    Waldorf: Chop apples and sprinkle with lemon juice. Add a dash of salt, chopped celery, and chopped pecans or walnuts; moisten with mayonnaise or salad dressing.

    Apple-Cold Meat Salad: Combine chopped cooked pork, ham, chicken or turkey, or tuna with equal amount of diced apples, some chopped celery, and mayonnaise or salad dressing to moisten.

    Cheese-Apple Salad: Combine three parts chopped apples with one part cubed cheese, some chopped celery, and salad dressing or mayonnaise to taste.

    Apple-Fruit Salads: Combinations of
- banana, pineapple tidbits, and apples
- strawberries, oranges, apples, and miniature marshmallows
- oranges, apples, and cranberry sauce
- banana, pitted cherries, apple, and orange

APPLE STUFFING

    ¼ *cup butter or margarine*
    ½ *cup onion, chopped*
    ½ *cup celery, chopped*
    4 *cups tart apples, diced*
    ½ *teaspoon salt*
    ⅓ *cup sugar*
    4 *cups soft bread crumbs*

In large skillet sauté onion, celery, and apples in butter. Sprinkle with salt and sugar. Cook, stirring occasionally, until apples are lightly browned. Add bread crumbs; toss gently to blend all ingredients. Use to stuff poultry, game, or pork.

APPLE SALAD MOLD

    1 *(6-ounce) package lemon gelatin*
    1½ *cups boiling water*
    2 *cups orange juice*
    1½ *cups cottage cheese*
    ½ *cup walnuts, finely chopped*
    2 *cups apples, peeled and diced*

Dissolve gelatin in boiling water. Add orange juice. Pour into 2-quart mold. Chill until partially set. Add remaining ingredients and chill until firm. Serves 6 to 8.

DOUBLE APPLE CAKE

> 4 cups fresh apples, chopped
> 2 cups sugar
> ½ cup vegetable oil
> 1 cup nuts, chopped (optional)
> 2 eggs
> 2 teaspoons vanilla
> 2 cups flour
> 2 teaspoons baking soda
> 2 teaspoons cinnamon
> 1 teaspoon salt

In large bowl combine sugar, oil, nuts, eggs, and vanilla. Combine dry ingredients; add to moist ingredients and blend well. Fold in apples and stir to coat apples completely with batter. Pour into 9-by-9-inch pan. Bake at 350° 50 to 60 minutes.

APPLE-SOUR CREAM PIE

> One 9-inch unbaked pie shell
> 2 cups apples, pared and sliced
> 2 tablespoons flour
> ¾ cup sugar
> 1 egg, beaten
> Pinch of salt
> 1 teaspoon vanilla
> 1 cup dairy sour cream
> ⅓ cup sugar
> ⅓ cup flour
> ¼ cup butter at room temperature
> 1 teaspoon cinnamon

In medium bowl combine 2 tablespoons flour, ¾ cup sugar, egg, salt, vanilla, and sour cream; stir in apples. Pour into unbaked pie shell. Bake at 350° 40 minutes. Rub together ⅓ cup sugar, ⅓ cup flour, butter, and cinnamon. Remove pie from oven; sprinkle on topping, then return to oven for 15 minutes. Serve warm or cold. Serves 6 to 8.

APPLESAUCE

How to Use: Use in applesauce cake, spice muffins, or coffeecakes.
Serve as accompaniment to pork roast, pork chops, or ham.
For a breakfast treat, heat and serve topped with butter and cinnamon.
Spread over cooked squash; bake until heated through.
Use as extender for meat loaf; add up to 1 cup applesauce to 2 pounds of ground meat; season with sage, onion, salt, pepper, and other seasonings as desired.
Serve with gingerbread or over unflavored yogurt.
Add up to 1 cup applesauce to a 3-ounce package of fruit-flavored gelatin.
For sandwich filling mix applesauce with peanut butter and crumbled cooked bacon; spread on bread. If desired top with thin apple slices and a second piece of bread.

APPLESAUCE BREAD

½ cup butter or margarine
1 cup sugar
2 eggs
1¾ cups flour
1 teaspoon salt
1 teaspoon baking powder
½ teaspoon baking soda
½ teaspoon cinnamon
½ teaspoon nutmeg
1 cup applesauce
½ cup nuts, finely chopped

Cream butter and sugar. Add eggs; beat until fluffy. Sift dry ingredients together; add to sugar-egg mixture alternately with applesauce. Stir in nuts. Pour into greased 9-by-5-by-3-inch loaf pan. Bake at 350° for 50 to 60 minutes. Cool in pan 10 minutes. Remove loaf and glaze with ½ cup powdered sugar mixed with about 1 tablespoon water.

APPLESAUCE MEAT LOAF

1 egg, slightly beaten
1 cup soft bread crumbs
½ cup applesauce
2 tablespoons onion, finely chopped
½ teaspoon celery salt

1 *teaspoon Dijon-style mustard*
½ *teaspoon salt*
   Dash pepper
1 *pound ground beef*

Topping:
   ½ *cup applesauce*
   1 *tablespoon brown sugar*
   1 *tablespoon vinegar*
   1 *teaspoon Dijon-style mustard*

In large bowl combine egg, bread crumbs, ½ cup applesauce, onion, celery salt, 1 teaspoon mustard, salt, and pepper; add beef and mix well. Pat into greased 8- or 9-inch square pan. Combine topping ingredients and spread over meat loaf. Bake at 350° for 1 hour. Serves 4 or 5.

APPLE-CINNAMON GELATIN MOLD

1 *(3-ounce) package lemon or cherry gelatin*
1 *cup boiling water*
½ *cup red cinnamon candy*
1 *cup applesauce*

In medium bowl mix cinnamon candies and gelatin. Pour on boiling water; stir to dissolve. Stir in applesauce. Pour into small mold or pan. Chill until set. Serves 4 to 6.

APPLESAUCE DROP COOKIES

1 *cup butter or margarine*
2 *cups sugar (use part brown sugar, if desired)*
⅛ *teaspoon salt*
1 *egg, beaten*
3 *cups flour*
1 *teaspoon cinnamon*
½ *teaspoon nutmeg*
½ *teaspoon baking soda*
1 *teaspoon baking powder*
1 *cup applesauce*
1 *cup wheat germ*
1 *teaspoon vanilla*
   Up to 1 cup chopped walnuts, raisins, or butterscotch chips,
      if desired

In large bowl cream butter, sugar, and salt. Beat in egg. Sift dry ingredients and beat into mixture. Add applesauce, vanilla, and wheat germ; mix thoroughly. (Batter will be stiff.) Add nuts, raisins, or chips. Drop batter by teaspoon onto greased cookie sheet. Bake at 375° for 12 to 15 minutes. Makes about 90 2-inch-diameter cookies.

AVOCADO

How to Use: Add to tossed green salads.

Cut avocado in chunks or wedges; dip in lemon juice and serve on salad greens with tomato wedges.

Blend seeded and peeled avocado with cream cheese, a small amount of lemon juice, and dry onion soup mix. Use for dip or to stuff tomatoes.

Serve slices on sandwiches made with dark bread. Top with seasoned cottage cheese.

Add sliced avocado to bacon, tomato, and lettuce sandwiches; serve open-face topped with Thousand Island dressing.

Use avocado slices as garnish for meat and fish platters; marinate avocado slices in French dressing, then roll in chopped parsley.

Avocado-fruit salads: Alternate avocado and grapefruit slices on salad greens, top with pomegranate seeds and sweet French dressing; or toss avocado chunks and orange sections with lettuce and fruit salad dressing; or coat avocado halves with lemon juice and fill with cranberry or lemon sherbet or with cantaloupe balls and strawberries. Alternate avocado and apple slices on greens and top with sweet French or celery seed dressing.

Stuff cold avocado halves with seafood salad.

Avocado salad dressing: Mix ½ of a mashed avocado with ½ cup French dressing until smooth.

Add mashed or pureed avocado to cream of chicken soup; season with onion salt, white pepper, and a little lemon juice. Serve hot or cold.

AVOCADO-EGG BRUNCH

½ cup mashed avocado
½ cup dairy sour cream
1 tablespoon lemon juice
1 teaspoon sugar

¼ *teaspoon salt*
¼ *teaspoon garlic powder*
   Dash Tabasco sauce
 1 *tomato, peeled and chopped*
 4 *eggs*
¼ *cup milk*
½ *teaspoon salt*
   Dash pepper
 2 *tablespoons vegetable oil*
¼ *cup onion, chopped*
 2 *English muffins, halved, toasted, and buttered*
 4 *slices tomato*

In small bowl combine avocado, sour cream, lemon juice, ¼ teaspoon salt, sugar, garlic powder, and Tabasco sauce. Fold in chopped tomato and set mixture aside. In separate bowl beat together eggs, milk, ½ teaspoon salt, and pepper. Heat oil in medium skillet; cook onion until transparent. Add egg mixture and cook, stirring gently, until eggs are barely set. Spread each muffin half with 1 tablespoon of the avocado mixture, ¼ of the scrambled eggs, and one slice of tomato. Top each serving with the remaining avocado mixture. Serves 4.

GUACAMOLE

 2 *ripe avocados, peeled and seeded*
 1 *tablespoon lemon juice*
½ *medium onion, grated*
 2 *tablespoons chili sauce*
   Dash Tabasco sauce

In small bowl mash avocado with fork until smooth. Blend in remaining ingredients. Chill in covered container. Use as dip for vegetables or crackers. Good also on broiled sandwiches topped with cheddar cheese.

TANGY AVOCADO DRESSING

½ *avocado, peeled and diced*
 1 *cup mayonnaise or salad dressing*
 1 *tablespoon onion, minced*
⅛ *teaspoon garlic salt*
1½ *teaspoons sugar*
1½ *teaspoons lemon juice*
¼ *teaspoon Worcestershire sauce*
½ *cup buttermilk*
   Dash hot pepper sauce, if desired

In medium bowl mix avocado with mayonnaise. Fold in onion, garlic salt, sugar, lemon juice, Worcestershire, hot pepper sauce, and buttermilk. Refrigerate several hours or overnight before using. Makes 2 cups dressing. Use within one week.

BANANAS

How to Use: Add mashed bananas to custards and gelatin desserts, using 1 banana to each 3 servings.

Add slices of banana to a peanut-butter sandwich.

Add to a cabbage salad made with shredded cabbage, diced apple, and chopped salted peanuts. Moisten with mayonnaise.

Banana snack: Spread chunks of banana with peanut butter. This makes a good-tasting but messy-to-eat children's snack.

Add to fruit-flavored gelatins with desired combinations of canned pineapple, apples, grapes, nuts, canned fruit cocktail, oranges, whipped cream, dairy sour cream, and so on.

Banana-fruit combinations for fruit salad or dessert: Use with any combination of the following: pineapple, green grapes, strawberries, cantaloupe, raspberries, orange sections, nuts, chopped dates, coconut, whipped cream, or dairy sour cream.

Banana salad dressing: Mash 1 banana with 1 tablespoon lemon juice; stir into ½ cup mayonnaise. Add 4 tablespoons peanut butter and ¼ cup evaporated milk. Serve over fresh fruit salads.

Blend with milk for a milk shake.

Use in banana cakes, banana breads, banana cream pies.

Top a baked banana cake with banana slices. Brush banana slices with lemon juice, then cover with a boiled white frosting.

Banana Sponge: In medium bowl add 1 cup boiling water to a 3-ounce package of lemon or orange gelatin; add ¾ cup cold water and chill until slightly thickened. Beat ½ cup chilled evaporated milk until stiff. To whipped milk add 2 tablespoons lemon juice, 2 tablespoons sugar, and 1 cup mashed bananas; beat slightly. Combine milk and gelatin mixtures. Pour into a 6-cup mold and chill until set. Serves 6.

Banana Shake: Combine in blender 2 medium-ripe bananas, ½ cup or more orange juice, and 1 to 2 tablespoons wheat germ, if desired. Blend at low speed until smooth. Makes two ½-cup servings.

BANANA PECAN CAKE

2½ cups flour
1 cup sugar
1¼ teaspoons baking powder
1¼ teaspoons baking soda
1 teaspoon salt
¾ cup butter, softened
⅔ cup buttermilk
1¼ cups very ripe bananas, mashed
2 eggs
½ cup pecans, chopped

In large bowl combine flour, sugar, baking powder, baking soda, and salt. Add butter, buttermilk, and bananas; beat until well moistened. Add eggs; beat 2 minutes. Stir in nuts. Place in 9-by-13-inch or 10-by-15-inch ungreased baking pan. Bake at 350° 30 to 40 minutes. Cool before frosting.

FROSTING:

4 cups powdered sugar
½ cup butter, softened
2 to 4 tablespoons milk
2 teaspoons vanilla
Pinch of salt
½ cup toasted pecans, chopped

In medium bowl combine sugar, butter, milk, vanilla, and salt. Beat with electric mixer at low speed, scraping sides of bowl frequently to blend in all ingredients. Beat on high speed until fluffy, about 1½ minutes. Fold in pecans. Spread over cake.

BERRIES

How to Use: Sweeten and serve on cold or hot cereals, puddings, or ice cream.
Crush and sweeten for toppings on pancakes, waffles, French toast, or buttered bread.

Use as garnishes.

Add to fruit plates and fruit salads.

Use in fruit cobblers.

Add to custard sauces.

Serve over fruit-flavored sherbet. Top with vanilla sauce, if desired.

Add pureed berries to whipped cream; serve over sherbet, ice cream, or cake.

Combine 2 cups pureed berries with ½ cup or more sugar, ½ cup dairy sour cream, 2 cups cold water, and ½ cup red wine. Chill and serve for a dessert or beverage.

Berry Gelatin Dessert: Drain juice from 2 cups cooked or frozen berries; use fruit juice as part of the liquid in making fruit-flavored gelatin according to package directions. When gelatin has partly set add berries. Chill until firm. Serve with whipped cream or topping.

Berry Shrub: In blender combine 1 to 2 cups fresh berries, 1 tablespoon honey, 2 cups milk, 1 tablespoon lemon juice, and a pinch of salt. Pour into tall glasses. Serves 4 to 6.

UNCOOKED BERRY SAUCE

Crush 1 pint berries in a bowl. Sweeten to taste. Let stand 2 hours in refrigerator. Strain, if desired.

COOKED BERRY SAUCE

In saucepan place 2 cups washed berries and ¼ cup water. Bring to a boil; cover and steam 5 to 7 minutes until berries are tender. Chill mixture, then sweeten to taste.

FRESH BERRY PIE

4 *cups fresh berries, cleaned and drained*
¾ *cup water*
1 *cup sugar*
3 *tablespoons cornstarch*
One 9-inch pie shell, baked
Whipped cream or whipped topping

In small saucepan simmer 1 cup berries in water for 3 minutes. Combine sugar and cornstarch; add to simmered berries and cook until thick. Cool mixture. Place the remaining 3 cups berries in pie shell; pour cooked berries over the uncooked berries. Chill. Cover pie with whipped cream before serving.

BAKED FRESH BERRY PIE

> 4 cups fresh berries
> 3 tablespoons quick-cooking tapioca or 2 tablespoons cornstarch
> ¼ cup water or fruit juice
> ⅔ to 1½ cups sugar
> 1 tablespoon lemon juice or ½ teaspoon cinnamon
> Pastry for a 2-crust pie

In medium bowl mix tapioca or cornstarch with water or fruit juice. Add sugar and berries. Flavor with lemon juice or cinnamon. Let mixture stand a few minutes to blend flavors. Pour into pie shell. Dot with butter. Cover with top crust; poke with fork or make slits in top crust with a sharp knife. Bake at 450° 10 minutes, then reduce heat to 350° and bake 40 to 45 minutes.

BERRY–SOUR CREAM PIE

> 1 cup sugar
> 1 cup dairy sour cream
> ¼ teaspoon salt
> 3 tablespoons flour
> 4 cups fresh or frozen berries (thawed)
> One 9-inch pie shell, unbaked
> ¼ cup fine dry bread crumbs
> 2 tablespoons sugar
> 1 tablespoon butter, melted

In small bowl combine 1 cup sugar, sour cream, salt, and flour. Place berries in pastry shell. Cover with sour-cream mixture. Combine bread crumbs, 2 tablespoons sugar, and melted butter; sprinkle over berries. Bake at 375° 40 to 45 minutes.

CANTALOUPE

How to Use: Cut into wedges or rings. Fill with fresh fruit or fruit-flavored sherbet or a combination of fruit and sherbet.
Mix cantaloupe balls or chunks with equal amounts of raspberries and orange juice.

Mix cantaloupe balls with honeydew and watermelon balls. Chill in orange juice.

Place a few cantaloupe balls in the center of a pineapple slice for a garnish.

Add cantaloupe balls to fruit-flavored gelatins along with such fruits as grapes, peaches, and pineapple.

Melon-Banana Compote: Combine cantaloupe and honeydew balls with banana slices. Cover with rhubarb sauce.

Cantaloupe Sundae: Cut cantaloupe into wedges. Fill wedges with ice cream. If desired, top with raspberry sauce or rhubarb sauce.

CANTALOUPE-LIME COOLER

> 3 *cups cantaloupe, diced*
> 1½ *cups cold water*
> 1 *tablespoon lime juice*
> 1 *teaspoon sugar*
> *Dash salt*
> *Lime slices, if desired*

In blender combine cantaloupe, water, lime juice, sugar, and salt; blend until smooth. Pour into chilled glasses. Garnish with lime slices, if desired. Makes 4 8-ounce servings.

KIRSCH CANTALOUPE

> 2 *tablespoons light corn syrup*
> 1 *tablespoon kirsch liqueur*
> ¼ *cup orange juice concentrate, undiluted*
> 4 *cups cantaloupe balls*
> *Fresh mint leaves, if desired*

In large bowl with tight-fitting cover, combine corn syrup, kirsch, and orange juice concentrate; blend well. Add melon balls. Cover bowl and shake gently to cover all melon balls with liquid. Refrigerate several hours before serving. Serve with fresh mint if desired. Serves 6.

CRANBERRIES

WHOLE CRANBERRY SAUCE

How to Use: Spoon on pear, peach, or avocado halves. Serve on lettuce leaves.

Spoon into orange or lemon shells to use as garnish for poultry.

Add up to 1 cup to a 3-ounce red fruit-flavored gelatin along with crushed pineapple, chopped walnuts, diced celery, and up to 1 cup dairy sour dream.

Fruit Salad Dressing: Combine ½ cup cranberry sauce, ¼ cup honey, and 1 teaspoon lemon juice. Chill before using.

Glaze for poultry or game birds: Combine 1 cup whole cranberry sauce, 2 tablespoons lemon juice, ½ cup brown sugar. Add during the last half-hour of cooking. Baste frequently.

Glaze for ham: Combine 1 cup whole cranberry sauce, ⅓ cup brown sugar, and a dash of nutmeg. Pour over a small ham during last 10 minutes of baking.

Add up to 1 to 2 cups baked beans before heating. Add cubed cooked ham, if desired.

Add up to 1 cup to Apple Crisp or Apple Crunch; reduce amount of apples accordingly.

JELLIED CRANBERRY SAUCE

How to Use: Slice and place on top of a lettuce leaf and pineapple slice.
Slice and serve with a topping of cole slaw.
Liquefy in blender and add to fruit juices or punch.

CRANBERRY-ORANGE RELISH

How to Use: Pile on peach, avocado, or pear halves and serve on salad greens.
Mound in orange shells for garnish.
Add up to 1¼ cups to 3 ounces of strawberry- or raspberry-flavored gelatin. Add drained pineapple tidbits and diced celery. Use 1 cup water in preparing gelatin.

CRANBERRY JUICE

How to Use: Add to fruit punch.
Mix with orange or apple juice and use as beverage.
Use up to 1½ cups cold cranberry juice for liquid in making a red fruit-flavored gelatin.
Use to poach fresh pears. Pour over peeled, halved, and cored pears; place in moderate oven 40 minutes.

RAW CRANBERRIES

How to Use: Chop and add up to 1 cup to muffins and quick breads before baking.

Use to make cranberry-orange relish. Grind 4 cups cranberries and 1 orange with its rind. Add 2 cups sugar. Chill two days before using.

Cook and add to fruit-flavored gelatins.

Make cranberry sauce: Place 4 cups washed cranberries in saucepan. Add 2 cups water, 2 cups sugar, and a dash of salt. Cover and bring to boil; simmer without stirring until all skins pop, about 5 minutes. Cool. Store in refrigerator.

Use in pies alone or with such fruit as blueberries, apples, and raisins, or in mince pie.

FRUIT JUICE

How to Use: Substitute for water in fruit-flavored or unflavored gelatins.

Add to punches and cold fruit drinks.

Freeze to make ice cubes for cold drinks.

Use in fruit cobblers, sherbets, tapioca, and rice pudding.

Freeze into popsicles; pour into plastic molds or ice cube trays and add wooden sticks for handles.

Use as glaze for roast ham or pork.

Fruit juice milk shake: Blend equal amounts of fruit juice and milk in blender. Add ripe bananas, if desired.

DESSERT SAUCE

> 1 *cup fruit juice*
> ½ *to* ¾ *cup sugar*
> 1 *tablespoon cornstarch*
> 2 *teaspoons lemon juice*
> 2 *tablespoons butter, if desired*
> 1 *cup fresh or cooked fruit, if desired*
> 1 *cup whipped topping, if desired*

Combine sugar and cornstarch. In heavy medium saucepan combine fruit juice with sugar mixture and mix well. Heat over moderate heat, stirring constantly until mixture is thick and clear. Remove from heat; stir in lemon juice and, if desired, butter. Add fresh fruit. Serve warm or cold over ice cream, fresh fruit, puddings, custards, and cakes. If sauce is to be served cold, whipped topping, if used, should be added just before serving.

MISCELLANEOUS FRUIT

How to Use: Use in fruit plates, fruit salads, and fruit compotes.

Add to fruit-flavored gelatins.

Crush to make sherbet.

Slice and serve with any of the following toppings: soft custard sauce, cream, whipped cream mixed with half the amount of dairy sour cream, or dairy sour cream mixed with brown sugar.

Marinate fresh fruit in such liqueurs as kirsch, Cointreau, or Grand Marnier. Peel and cut up fruit; toss with lemon juice, sugar, and grated lemon or orange rind. Add liqueur to taste. Chill several hours before serving.

Fruit Milk Shakes: Add 1 cup cut fruit to 2 cups milk. If desired, add honey or sugar, and vanilla or almond flavoring. Shake to mix or whirl in blender.

Fresh Fruit Tarts: Drop fresh fruit into melted currant jelly. Pile into baked tart shells. Serve immediately.

FRESH FRUIT SAUCE

Steam 2 pounds of pitted and chopped fresh fruit in ½ cup boiling water until soft, about 15 minutes. Press through colander or food mill. Season to taste with nutmeg, cinnamon, lemon juice, grated lemon or orange rind, honey or sugar. Serve over ice cream, sherbet, custards, or pudding.

QUICK FRUIT TAPIOCA

> 2½ cups fruit juice and water
> ½ cup sugar
> ¼ cup quick-cooking tapioca
> ¼ teaspoon salt
> 1½ to 2 cups fruit, cut and drained, optional (use resulting fruit juice as part of the 2½ cups fruit juice)

In medium saucepan combine fruit juice, sugar, tapioca, and salt. Cook over medium heat, stirring constantly, until mixture boils. Remove from heat; cool. Fold in cut fruit. Serves 6.

FRESH FRUIT COBBLER

3 *cups fresh fruit, covered with any fruit juice*
⅔ *to 1 cup sugar*
1 *tablespoon cornstarch*
1 *cup water*
½ *tablespoon butter*
½ *teaspoon cinnamon*
   Dash nutmeg, if desired
   Shortcake dough or prepared biscuit mix dough

In medium saucepan mix sugar and cornstarch. Add water gradually. Bring to a boil; boil 1 minute, stirring constantly. Add fruit. Pour into 8-inch square baking dish. Dot with butter; sprinkle with cinnamon. Cover with favorite shortcake dough or prepared biscuit mix. Bake at 400° for 30 minutes. Serves 6.

FROZEN FRUIT DESSERT

2 *pounds fresh fruit (plums, apricots, nectarines, peaches),*
   pitted and sliced
1½ *to 2 cups granulated sugar*
4 *egg yolks*
1¾ *cups powdered sugar*
¼ *cup orange juice or orange-flavored liqueur*
2 *cups whipped topping or whipped cream*

In medium saucepan combine fruit and granulated sugar. Stir over low heat until sugar is dissolved. Heat to boiling. Cover and simmer until tender. Puree, then cool. In medium bowl beat egg yolks and powdered sugar until mixture is very thick. Add orange juice or liqueur slowly, beating constantly. Beat 5 minutes. Add whipped topping; beat 2 minutes. Stir fruit puree into mixture, stirring only enough to give mixture a marbleized appearance; do not mix completely. Freeze until a few minutes before serving. Spoon into small dessert dishes or sherbet dishes. Serves 10 to 12.

USE-IT-UP COOKIES

1 *cup fruits, nuts, or cooked carrots or squash*
1½ *cups flour*
1½ *teaspoons baking powder*
¼ *teaspoon salt*

¾ *cup shortening*
1 *cup sugar*
1 *egg, beaten*
1 *teaspoon vanilla*

Prepare fruits and nuts by cutting into small pieces. Peel fruits with skins; save fruit juice. In large bowl combine flour, baking powder, and salt. Cut in shortening and blend well. Add sugar, egg, and vanilla. Stir in fruits and nuts. If batter is too stiff, thin with fruit juice. Drop by spoonfuls onto greased baking sheets. Bake at 350° 15 minutes. Makes 36 cookies.

GRAPEFRUIT

How to Use: Fresh fruit salad combinations: Place grapefruit sections on salad greens and serve with sweet French dressing. Or alternate grapefruit sections with avocado slices and top with pomegranate seeds and sweet French dressing. Or alternate peach slices and grapefruit sections and sprinkle with flaked coconut. Or alternate orange sections and grapefruit sections on greens and serve with honey-fruit dressing.

Arrange grapefruit sections and thin slices of sweet onions on salad greens; serve with French dressing.

Add grapefruit and grated carrots to lemon gelatin for a molded salad.

Add to orange-flavored gelatin along with orange sections and seedless grapes. Add a dash of salt and 2 tablespoons lemon juice. If desired, add diced celery and chopped apples.

Use grapefruit sections in lime-flavored gelatin along with diced celery, pecans, crushed pineapple, cottage cheese, and a dash of salt.

Sweeten grapefruit sections with maple syrup or honey; broil and serve for breakfast.

Spiced Fruit Cup: In saucepan combine 1 cup each grapefruit and orange sections with membranes removed (reserve juice), 1 stick cinnamon, a dash each of cloves and ginger, and reserved fruit juice. Bring to a boil, then simmer 10 minutes. Remove cinnamon and chill.

Grapefruit juice: Use in place of cold water in preparing fruit-flavored gelatins or in aspics.

GRAPEFRUIT MOLDED SALAD

> 2 *tablespoons unflavored gelatin*
> ½ *cup cold water*
> 1½ *cups boiling water*
> 1½ *cups grapefruit juice*
> ½ *to 1 cup sugar*
> 3 *to 4 cups grapefruit sections, with skin and membranes removed*

Optional Topping:
> 6 *ounces cream cheese at room temperature*
> ¼ *cup light cream or evaporated milk*
> ⅓ *cup walnuts, chopped*

In a cup, soften gelatin in ½ cup cold water. Pour boiling water into large bowl; add gelatin mixture and stir until gelatin is dissolved. Add grapefruit juice and sugar to taste. Add grapefruit sections; pour into serving dish. Refrigerate until firm. If desired, frost with cream cheese topping. Mix cream cheese and cream until smooth; spread over gelatin. Sprinkle nuts over top. Serves 10 to 12.

PIQUANT MOLDED SALAD

> 1 *(3-ounce) package lime, lemon, or orange-flavored gelatin*
> 1 *teaspoon salt*
> 1 *cup boiling water*
> ¾ *cup cold water (can use part grapefruit juice)*
> 2 *teaspoons lemon juice*
> 1 *grapefruit, sectioned, diced and drained (reserve juice)*
> 1 *apple, diced*
> 2 *tablespoons pecans, chopped*
> 3 *tablespoons ripe olives, sliced*

In medium bowl dissolve gelatin and salt in boiling water. Add cold water, grapefruit juice, and lemon juice. Chill until partially set. Fold in grapefruit, apple, olives, and nuts. Pour into 4-cup mold. Chill 4 hours or until firm. Serves 6.

LEMON

How to Use: Sprinkle lemon juice over vegetables as a seasoning.
Substitute lemon juice for vinegar in making salad dressing.
Add to tomato juice to enhance flavor.
Sprinkle lemon juice over tossed salads.
Use in Greek Lemon Soup (Avgolemono).

Lemon Butter: Melt ¼ cup butter; add juice from 1 lemon. Serve over cooked vegetables. Add chopped parsley or chives, if desired. Other herbs to include are marjoram, thyme, or mint. Or add nutmeg or ground ginger.

Lemon Garnishes:

A lemon wedge sprinkled with paprika to accompany fish.

A thin lemon slice topped with a thin slice of unpeeled cucumber for garnishing hot or cold fish fillets.

A lemon section coated with finely chopped parsley or watercress for seafood.

A lemon shell with fluted edges filled with cranberry sauce for poultry garnish.

PEACHES

How to Use: Serve peach halves filled with cottage cheese or cream cheese balls rolled in chopped nuts. Serve on salad greens.

Add to fruit salads.

Slice, dip in lemon juice, and use for garnish along with cherries and green grapes.

Halve peaches, brush with lemon juice, and fill with sweetened berries.

Steam or poach for peach sauce.

Add sliced peaches to peach-flavored gelatin. Add blueberries and green grapes, if desired.

Diced sweetened peaches may be served over cereals, pudding, or ice cream.

Slice and mix with fresh strawberries. (Coat fresh peaches with a little lemon juice to keep them from darkening.)

Chill peach slices in orange juice sweetened with honey. Add a dash of salt and chopped candied ginger. Serve in sherbet glasses.

Puree and add to punch or fruit juices.

Slice, sprinkle with sugar, and top with light cream for a quick dessert.

Use in pies and cobblers.

Peaches and Cream: Layer slices of peaches and dairy sour cream sprinkled with brown sugar in sherbet glasses. Use 3 layers of fruit and sour cream. Serve at once.

Add up to 1 ½ cups mashed peaches to quick breads.

Use in the classic Peach Melba or Peaches Cardinal desserts.

Quick Peach Melba: Top poached peach halves with vanilla ice cream and cover with raspberry sauce.

PEARS

How to Use: Use pear halves brushed with lemon juice and filled with a mixture of berries or cream cheese balls for a salad. Serve on salad greens.

Add pears to Waldorf salad.

Slice, brush with lemon or orange juice, and toss with sliced celery. Arrange on salad greens. Top with a fruit salad dressing.

Add pear slices, onion, and brown sugar to sauerkraut before baking.

Baked pears: Place sliced pears and canned pineapple chunks in baking dish. Sprinkle with sugar, lemon juice, ¼ cup pineapple juice, and a sprinkling of ground cloves. Bake at 350° 1 hour.

Pear Compote: Combine 3 pears cut into chunks with 1 sliced apple, 1 cup grapes, 2 sliced bananas, and 1 peeled and diced avocado. Toss with ¼ cup honey and 2 tablespoons orange juice concentrate. Chill before serving. Serves 6.

GINGERBREAD-PEAR CAKE

1 *(14-ounce) package gingerbread mix*
½ cup orange juice
2 cups pears, sliced
⅓ cup walnuts or almonds, chopped or thinly sliced
2 tablespoons butter, melted

Combine gingerbread mix and orange juice; beat 2 minutes. Fold in pears and spread mixture in greased 9-inch baking pan. Sprinkle with nuts. Pour butter evenly over top. Bake at 375° 25 to 35 minutes. Serve warm with whipped topping or ice cream. Serves 9.

PINEAPPLE, CANNED

PINEAPPLE CHUNKS OR TIDBITS

How to Use: Add to gelatins along with fruit combinations or with such vegetables as shredded carrots, cabbage, or green pepper.

Pineapple Waldorf Salad: Combine pineapple chunks with

sliced celery and chopped walnuts. Moisten with mayonnaise. Add lemon juice and salt to taste.

Pineapple-Banana Salad: Arrange chilled pineapple chunks and sliced bananas in serving dish. Top with a small amount of pineapple juice. Garnish with salad greens.

Pineapple-Cucumber Relish: Combine pineapple with diced cucumbers, dairy sour cream, honey, and lemon juice. Serve on salad greens.

Orange-Pineapple-Coconut Salad: Combine 1 cup orange segments, ¾ cup drained pineapple chunks, ⅓ cup chopped walnuts, 1 cup flaked coconut, and ½ cup dairy sour cream. Chill before serving. Serves 4.

Shred or mince and use in recipes calling for crushed pineapple.

Add to baked beans. Season to taste with vinegar, brown sugar or molasses, bacon, onions, dry mustard, chili sauce, salt, and pepper. Add frankfurters or cubed cooked ham, if desired.

Add to Rice au Gratin; serve with ham slices.

Pour light-flavored wine over pineapple; chill before serving for dessert.

Use in place of apples in Apple Betty.

Marinate in crème de menthe thinned with pineapple juice. Serve with lime sherbet.

Baked Pineapple Dessert: Place canned pears in baking dish, reserving pear liquid. Cover with canned pineapple and grated orange rind. Sprinkle lightly with sugar and ground cloves. Add reserved juice to fill pan halfway to top. Bake at 350° 1 hour.

PINEAPPLE-CHEESE BAKE

1 to 1½ cups pineapple chunks or tidbits (reserve juice)
¼ cup flour
¼ cup sugar
4 ounces cheddar cheese, sliced

Place drained pineapple chunks in greased baking dish. Sprinkle with flour and sugar. Cover with slices of cheese; sprinkle with pineapple juice. Bake uncovered at 350° for 45 minutes, stirring occasionally. If desired, place slices of cooked ham over pineapple-cheese mixture after 30 minutes and continue baking until ham is heated through. Or serve mixture as a side dish with baked ham or pork. Serves 3 or 4.

CRUSHED PINEAPPLE

How to Use: Add crushed pineapple to mayonnaise; spoon over fruit salads.

Mix with small pieces of prunes and spoon over cottage cheese on lettuce.

Mix with grated raw carrots and chopped toasted walnuts. Moisten with mayonnaise, if desired. Serve on lettuce leaves.

Curried Sour Cream Sauce: Add crushed pineapple to dairy sour cream, flavor with curry powder, and serve over slices of cold chicken or cold cooked rice.

Add to grated cabbage. Moisten with mayonnaise thinned with pineapple juice.

Squash stuffing: Mix drained pineapple with honey, cinnamon, nutmeg, chopped walnuts, and enough pineapple juice to moisten. Spoon into acorn squash halves which are nearly baked. Return to oven and bake 15 minutes or until squash is tender.

Add to fruit dressings for stuffing ham or pork roasts.

Sprinkle over cooked winter squash along with butter, brown sugar, and salt.

Pineapple Frosting: Cream 3 tablespoons butter with 2½ cups powdered sugar, 1 tablespoon lemon juice, and ¼ cup drained pineapple. Add enough pineapple juice to make of desired consistency.

PINEAPPLE-LIME SALAD MOLD

1 *(3-ounce) package lime gelatin*
1¼ *cups boiling water*
½ *cup stuffed olives, sliced*
½ *cup dairy sour cream*
1 *cup crushed pineapple, drained*
½ *cup celery, minced*

Dissolve gelatin in boiling water; chill. When partially set, fold in olives, sour cream, pineapple, and celery. Chill until set. Serves 6.

PINEAPPLE SLICES

How to Use: Sauté with thin ham slices; serve over waffles or French toast.

Top a cooked hamburger patty with sliced pineapple; brush

with pineapple juice and brown under broiler.

Use as base for cottage cheese, chicken, turkey or tuna salad, or baked ham balls.

Place on top of baked ham loaf for garnish, during last few minutes of baking.

Use to garnish fruit salad plates. Fill center of slices with berries, grapes, melon balls, or orange sections.

Cover with strawberry ice cream and top with orange liqueur.

PINEAPPLE JUICE

How to Use: Serve hot as an appetizer.

Spice and heat as for hot spiced apple juice.

Use as part of liquid in making fruit-flavored gelatins or in fruit aspics.

Fruit Salad Dressing: Combine ¼ cup pineapple juice, ½ cup dairy sour cream, a dash salt, 1 teaspoon lemon juice, and 1 tablespoon sugar. Chill before using.

Use in cooked white frostings in place of water.

PINEAPPLE-BUTTERMILK COOLER

2 *cups buttermilk*
2 *cups pineapple juice*
1½ *to 2 teaspoons sugar*
 Fresh mint for garnish

In pitcher combine buttermilk, pineapple juice, and sugar. Chill. Garnish with mint. Serves 4.

POMEGRANATE

How to Use: Wash pomegranate. Cut or break in half carefully. Try not to squeeze seed kernels while breaking, as the juice spatters. Remove seed kernels carefully with fork or fingers.

Use seeds for garnish on fruit salads, fruit compotes, or fruit desserts.

Add to sweet French dressing for fruit salads.

Roll seed kernels in small balls of cream cheese and serve over pineapple slices, or pear or peach halves.

Eat seed kernels alone as a snack or dessert.

PUMPKIN

How to Use: Unseasoned cooked pumpkin can be substituted in equal amounts in recipes calling for winter squash.

Use to make pumpkin soup.

Add up to ½ cup cooked pumpkin to muffin batter; add cinnamon and nutmeg, and if desired, raisins.

Add 1 cup cooked pumpkin and 1 cup cold milk to a 3-ounce package of vanilla instant pudding. Add ½ teaspoon cinnamon, ½ teaspoon allspice, and ¼ teaspoon nutmeg. Beat until pudding thickens. Pour into serving dishes and chill 15 minutes. Serves 6.

PUMPKIN COOKIES

¼ cup shortening
½ cup sugar
1 egg, beaten
½ cup cooked pumpkin
½ teaspoon vanilla
1 cup flour
2 teaspoons baking powder
½ teaspoon salt
½ teaspoon cinnamon
¼ teaspoon nutmeg
½ cup raisins
½ cup nuts, chopped

Cream shortening and sugar together. Add egg; beat thoroughly. Stir in pumpkin and vanilla. Sift dry ingredients together; blend into pumpkin mixture. Stir in raisins and nuts. Drop by teaspoonfuls about 2 inches apart on greased baking sheet. Bake at 350° 15 minutes or until lightly browned. Makes 2 dozen.

PUMPKIN BARS

4 eggs, well beaten
1⅔ cups sugar
1 cup vegetable oil
2 cups cooked pumpkin
2 cups flour
2 teaspoons baking powder
1 teaspoon baking soda

2 *teaspoons cinnamon*
Dash salt

FROSTING:
  1 *(3-ounce) package cream cheese, softened*
  4 *tablespoons butter or margarine, softened*
  1 *tablespoon milk or cream*
  1 *teaspoon vanilla*
  2 *cups powdered sugar*

Combine eggs, sugar, oil, and pumpkin in large bowl; beat until well blended. Mix the dry ingredients together well and add to the pumpkin mixture. Pour into greased 10-by-15-inch baking pan. Bake at 350° 25 to 30 minutes. Cool before frosting. To make frosting, beat cream cheese, butter, milk, and vanilla until fluffy. Add sugar gradually, blending until smooth. Makes about 40 bars.

RHUBARB

How to Use: Quick Rhubarb Snack: Dip a stalk of freshly picked and cleaned rhubarb into sugar, then eat it. Do not eat rhubarb leaves, as they are poisonous.

Rhubarb-Pineapple Juice: Liquefy 1 cup diced rhubarb in blender with 1½ cups pineapple juice, sugar or honey to taste, and ice.

Rhubarb Juice: Cook rhubarb in a small amount of water until tender. Strain off juice and store in covered bottle in refrigerator. Add juice to tea or cold beverages. Juice may also be used for rhubarb jelly.

Quick Baked Rhubarb: Place 6 cups of ½-inch sections of rhubarb stalks in greased baking dish. Combine ½ cup orange juice and ¾ cup sugar; sprinkle over rhubarb. Cover and bake at 300° 30 minutes. Serve with poultry, pork, or lamb.

No-Stir Rhubarb Sauce: Boil together ½ cup water and 2 cups sugar for 6 minutes. Add 6 cups rhubarb stalks, cut in 1½-inch pieces. Bring to boil; cover. Remove from heat and let cool. Serve plain or with cream. Or use as topping for ice cream or shortcake. Or add up to ¾ cup to a red fruit-flavored gelatin.

Use in Rhubarb Crisp or Rhubarb Crumble.

Substitute rhubarb for apples in Apple Brown Betty. Use white sugar instead of brown sugar, and omit water.

COOKED RHUBARB SAUCE

4 *cups rhubarb, cut into 1-inch pieces*
¾ *to 1 cup sugar*
2 *to 4 tablespoons water*

In heavy saucepan with cover, combine all ingredients. Cook over medium heat until mixture simmers slowly. Cover and continue simmering until rhubarb falls apart when stirred. Pour into covered container and store in refrigerator. Makes about 2 cups sauce. Use sauce as topping for cakes, applesauce, or ice cream.

BAKED RHUBARB PUDDING

3 *cups rhubarb, chopped*
1 *egg, beaten*
¾ *cup sugar*
2 *tablespoons flour*
¼ *cup butter or margarine*
½ *cup brown sugar*
1 *cup graham cracker crumbs*

In medium bowl, beat egg; add rhubarb, sugar, and flour. Pour into greased 8-inch square baking pan. Combine butter, brown sugar, and crumbs; sprinkle over rhubarb mixture. Bake at 350° 35 to 45 minutes. Serve warm. Serves 6.

RHUBARB CAKE AS-YOU-LIKE-IT

1½ *cups brown sugar*
½ *cup butter*
1 *egg*
1 *teaspoon vanilla*
1 *cup buttermilk*
2 *cups flour*
½ *teaspoon salt*
1 *teaspoon baking soda*
¼ *teaspoon allspice, if desired*
¼ *teaspoon ground cloves, if desired*
1 *teaspoon cinnamon, if desired*
½ *cup chopped nuts, if desired*
1½ *to 2 cups diced raw rhubarb*

In large bowl cream sugar and butter together. Add egg and vanilla; blend well. Sift together the flour, salt, baking soda, and seasonings. Add to the egg mixture alternately with the buttermilk. Stir in rhubarb and nuts, if desired. Pour into a greased 9-by-13-inch pan. Add desired topping.

TOPPING MIXTURES:
    ⅓ cup sugar and 1 teaspoon cinnamon, or
    ½ cup powdered sugar and 1 teaspoon cinnamon, or
        Either of the above toppings plus ¼ cup diced raw rhubarb

Bake at 350° 40 to 45 minutes. Serve warm as a coffeecake or serve cool with whipped cream or ice cream as a dessert.

RHUBARB BARS

    1½ cups flour
    1 teaspoon baking powder
    ½ teaspoon salt
    ½ cup butter or margarine
    1 egg, beaten
    1 tablespoon milk
    2 cups rhubarb, cut up
    1 (3-ounce) package strawberry gelatin
    1 cup sugar

In medium bowl, combine flour, baking powder, and salt; cut in butter. Set aside ½ cup for topping. Add egg and milk to mixture in bowl; mix well. Pat mixture into an 8-inch square pan. Place rhubarb on crust; sprinkle with strawberry gelatin. Add 1 cup sugar to reserved topping mixture; sprinkle over fruit. Bake at 350° for 45 to 50 minutes. Serve warm with ice cream or serve cool as bars. Cut into bars before completely cool.

RHUBARB-CUSTARD PIE

    2 eggs, beaten
    1 cup sugar
    2 tablespoons flour
    ¼ teaspoon salt
    2 cups rhubarb, finely chopped
        One unbaked 9-inch pie shell
    ½ cup brown sugar
    2 tablespoons flour
    2 tablespoons butter, melted

In medium bowl beat eggs well. Add sugar, 2 tablespoons flour, and salt. Add rhubarb and stir until rhubarb is well coated. Pour into pie shell. In separate bowl combine brown sugar, 2 tablespoons flour, and melted butter; sprinkle over rhubarb mixture. Bake at 400° 15 minutes; reduce temperature to 350° and bake 30 minutes.

WATERMELON

How to Use: Cut watermelon into chunks or slices for a fruit plate or to accompany a cold plate of chicken or seafood salad.

For garnish, make watermelon balls and place in the center of pineapple slices.

Watermelon Cooler: Combine 2 cups seeded and cubed watermelon with 2 teaspoons lemon juice and a dash of salt. Puree in blender. Pour over ice cubes in tall glasses. Serves 3.

Melon-Wine Compote: Combine melon balls made from watermelon, cantaloupe, and honeydew melon. Cover with white wine and chill 1 hour. Add green and red grapes and fresh cherries. Garnish with mint leaves.

Watermelon Compote: Combine 4 cups watermelon balls, 2 cups cantaloupe balls, 1 (13-ounce) can pineapple chunks, 3 large apples cut in wedges, and mint leaves. Chill several hours before serving.

Watermelon Bowl: Cut a chilled watermelon in half lengthwise. If desired, cut edge, using a sawtooth or zigzag line. Using a melon-ball cutter, remove as much whole pulp as possible. Remove remaining seeds and pulp separately and set aside. Combine watermelon balls with balls made of honeydew and cantaloupe. If desired, add sliced peaches, seedless grapes, pineapple tidbits, and whole strawberries. Place fruit in watermelon shell. Serve at once.

Miscellaneous

BROTH

BEEF BROTH

How to Use: Use to thin gravies.

Use as liquid for cooking vegetables and dried peas or beans.

Add to stews or pot roasts as part of cooking liquid.

Use as part of cooking liquid when preparing spaghetti, noodles, rice, or macaroni.

Combine with tomato juice and heat; serve hot in mugs or bowls.

Use as base for French onion soup or vegetable soup.

Add to chow mein or Jambalaya.

Quick Brown Sauce: Heat 1 cup beef broth to simmering. Mix ¼ cup broth in small jar or cup with 1½ tablespoons cornstarch; stir mixture into hot broth and cook 1 minute. Season to taste. Add cubed meat or cooked vegetables. Serve over rice, noodles, or toast.

QUICK BORDELAISE SAUCE

1 *tablespoon onion, minced*
½ *clove garlic, minced*
2 *teaspoons butter*
¼ *cup mushrooms, chopped (optional)*
1½ *tablespoons cornstarch*
1 *cup beef broth*
1 *teaspoon tomato paste*
1½ *tablespoons red wine*
1 *tablespoon lemon juice*
¼ *teaspoon pepper*
1 *tablespoon parsley, chopped*
Salt to taste

In small saucepan sauté onions and garlic in butter until brown. Add mushrooms and sauté briefly. Combine cornstarch and beef broth. Blend into vegetable mixture; cook and stir until mixture boils. Add remaining ingredients; simmer 5 minutes. Makes about 1 cup sauce. Serve with steaks, chops, or grilled meat.

RICE PILAF

> 2 *tablespoons vegetable oil*
> 1 *cup onion, chopped*
> ⅓ *cup fresh parsley, chopped*
> 1 *clove garlic, minced*
> 1 *cup raw brown or white rice*
> 2 *cups beef broth, heated to boiling*
> 1 *teaspoon salt*
> *Dash pepper*
> ½ *to 1 cup sliced mushrooms or chopped tomatoes, if desired*
> 2 *tablespoons Parmesan cheese, grated*

In skillet or saucepan with tight-fitting cover, sauté onions, parsley, garlic, and rice in oil until rice is golden. Add hot broth and seasonings. Add mushrooms or tomatoes, if desired; stir well. Cover tightly and cook over low heat 1 hour or until rice is tender. Add more broth if needed. Fluff lightly with a fork and sprinkle with Parmesan cheese before serving. Serves 4 to 6.

CHICKEN BROTH

How to Use: Use as a base for many cream soups, vegetable soups, and bisques.

Use to thin gravies.

Use as cooking liquid for vegetables, spaghetti, noodles, and rice.

Chicken broth is used in such classic dishes as French onion soup, Greek Lemon Soup, Vichyssoise, and Coq au Vin.

Cream of Pea Soup: Combine broth with cooked peas that have been pureed in blender.

CHICKEN BROTH

Strip excess cooked meat from chicken bones. Place bones and skin in large kettle; add enough water to barely cover. Add salt, peppercorns, whole allspice, onions, celery stalks and leaves, and a whole carrot. If desired, substitute dried vegetable flakes for the fresh vegetables. Or flavor with seasoned salt or herbs and seasonings of choice. Bring to boil. Reduce heat, cover, and simmer 1½ hours. Cool. Remove meat from bones. Strain broth and store in covered containers in refrigerator; use within two days. Or freeze and store for up to three months.

CHICKEN NOODLE SOUP

Add 1 cup uncooked noodles to 1 quart chicken broth. Cook 10 to 15 minutes.

CHICKEN RICE SOUP

Add ¼ cup raw rice to 3 cups chicken broth. Cook 20 to 25 minutes, or until rice is tender.

CHICKEN GUMBO SOUP

Sauté green pepper, okra, and onion in vegetable oil. Add to 3 cups chicken broth. Add 4 large tomatoes, peeled and chopped, 1 bay leaf, salt and pepper to taste. If desired, add cooked chopped ham, diced cooked chicken, chopped parsley, or cooked rice. Simmer 15 minutes.

MULLIGATAWNY SOUP

> 1 *medium onion, diced*
> 1 *carrot, diced*
> 1 *stalk celery, diced*
> 2 *tablespoons vegetable oil*
> 3 *tablespoons flour*
> ½ *to 1 teaspoon curry powder*
>   *Dash of mace and ground cloves*
> 2 *cups chicken broth*
> 1 *apple, diced*
> 1 *cup cooked chicken, cubed*
>   *Salt and pepper*
> 2 *chopped tomatoes, if desired*
> ⅓ *cup cooked rice, if desired*

In large saucepan sauté onion, carrot, and celery in oil. Stir in flour, curry powder, mace, and cloves. Add chicken broth and diced apple; simmer 30 minutes. Add chicken. Season to taste with salt and pepper. If desired, add tomatoes and rice. Heat until warmed through. Serves 6.

HAM BROTH

How to Use: Use for part of liquid when making lentil soup, potato soup, or split-pea soup. Use less salt than recipe calls for.
Add to stews, Jambalaya, or beans with rice dishes.
Add to gravies.

USE-IT-UP CHOWDER

½ medium onion, chopped
2 tablespoons bacon fat or vegetable oil
¼ cup green pepper, chopped (optional)
2 cups ham broth, or other meat or vegetable broth
1 to 2 cups raw or cooked potatoes, chopped
1 to 2 cups cooked vegetables, if desired
½ to 1 cup cooked meat, chopped
Salt and pepper to taste

In medium saucepan sauté onion and green pepper in bacon fat until onion is transparent. Add broth or water and potatoes; cook until potatoes are tender. Add cooked vegetables or meat; heat until warmed through. Season to taste. To obtain desired consistency, either thin with milk or thicken with a flour-water paste. Serves 4 to 6.

VEGETABLE BROTH (includes liquid from canned vegetables and vegetable-cooking water)

How to Use: Use as liquid for making gravies.
Use as soup base.
Use broth from mild-flavored vegetables for cooking spaghetti, noodles, or macaroni.
Use as liquid for cooking pot roast.
Add to stews or Jambalaya.
Freeze small quantities of juice until you have enough for soup. You may add liquid vegetable juice to frozen juice in the carton until carton is filled to 1 inch from the top.

COCONUT

How to Use: Use in fruit salads.

Five-Cup Salad: Combine 1 cup each of drained pineapple chunks, drained mandarin oranges, flaked coconut, miniature marshmallows, and dairy sour cream. Chill before serving.

Add to waffle batter before baking.

Add to fudge, cake fillings, dessert sauce, or to cream or custard pies.

Use in macaroons, coconut cake, or in drop cookies.

Use in Ambrosia.

Sprinkle over cooked white frostings.

FROSTING

How to Use: Spread on graham crackers or cookies.

Spoon over ice cream or puddings.

Use on pastry tarts.

Frosted Strawberries: Dip washed unhulled strawberries in butter frosting, then dip in shredded coconut.

GARNISHES

A simple garnish can brighten up an ordinary meal and make it more appealing to the eye and palate. These Use-It-Up garnishes offer an easy way to make the best use of what you have on hand.

GARNISHES MADE OF VEGETABLES

Carrot sticks, slivers, or curls
Celery stalks with leaves
Radish roses with romaine leaves and ripe olives
Cauliflower flowerets
Cherry tomatoes with parsley, celery sticks, or pickles
Pitted ripe olives stuffed with carrot sticks
Sliced cucumbers with fork-fluted edges
Cole slaw piled on tomato or cooked beet slices
Thin cucumber slices on top of lemon slices for seafood
Green-pepper ring and onion ring

Carrots cut in crosswise slices with center cores removed and a sprig of
    parsley or watercress inserted into the opening
Small whole beets or beet slices on greens
Endive stuffed with Roquefort or seasoned creamed cheese
Red bell pepper and green-pepper rings
Avocado wedges dipped in lemon juice and tomato wedges placed on greens
Cooked asparagus stalks in a ring of green pepper or on orange slices
Leaves of dark green lettuce or shredded lettuce
Whole or sliced or chopped olives
Watercress or parsley sprigs
Pickled Brussels sprouts

GARNISHES MADE OF FRUIT

Pineapple slice filled with mandarin orange sections or melon balls
Cranberry relish or whole cranberry sauce in pear halves or avocado halves.
    Serve in lettuce cups.
Spiced crab apples and watercress or endive
Pickled peach half and celery sprig with leaves
Coleslaw heaped on jellied cranberry slice
Cooked cranberries in fluted orange shells
Apricot halves heated in butter, dusted with nutmeg, and edged with parsley
Lemon slices or wedges coated with chopped parsley for seafood
Peach half filled with cottage cheese or cream cheese ball topped with
    chopped walnuts
Pear halves topped with mayonnaise and shredded cheddar cheese
Lemon slice pierced with parsley sprig
Small bunches of red or green grapes
Orange slices or wedges
Thin slices of lemons, limes, or oranges arranged in attractive pattern

GARNISHES FOR SOUP

Grated cheese
Chopped parsley
Chopped hard-cooked egg
Chopped fresh dill
Lemon slice
Cucumber slices
Sliced green onion
Crisp bacon bits
Fresh mint
Round slices of radish

Crumbled crackers or potato chips
Thin rounds of frankfurters or sausage
Chopped ripe olives
Toast rounds or croutons
Thinly sliced celery
Chopped chives
Onion rings
Chopped nuts
Shredded carrots
Sieved egg yolk
Thinly sliced strips of ham, beef, or lunch meat

GRAVY

How to Use: Serve warmed gravy over bread topped with cooked meat slices.

Heat diced cooked potatoes in gravy; season to taste.

Heat and serve over hot cooked rice.

Add chopped meat and serve over potatoes, noodles, or rice. Sautéed mushrooms or onions may be added. Thin with milk or broth, if desired.

Add gravy to such soups as vegetable, pea, or bean.

Add to stuffing mixture when making stuffed vegetables.

Tender baked liver: Dip liver slices into seasoned flour and brown lightly on both sides. Fry a large sliced onion. Arrange liver and onions in a baking dish. Pour 1½ to 3 cups gravy over liver and onions. Cover and bake at 350° for 45 minutes or until tender.

Schnitzel Sauce: Add sautéed bacon and golden-fried onions to gravy. Heat, add a small amount of dairy sour cream, and serve over fried pork or veal chops.

HONEY

How to Use: Substitute for sugar in recipes by using 1 cup honey for 1 cup sugar and reducing liquid in recipe by ¼ cup. (For cakes, substitute honey for only half the sugar. For cakes, cookies, and quick breads, add ¼ teaspoon baking soda for each cup honey and decrease baking powder by 1 teaspoon or to a minimum of ½ teaspoon.)

Use to sweeten tea.

Glaze for pork roast: ½ cup honey, ½ cup soy sauce, and 1 tablespoon dry mustard.

Glaze for ham: Pour honey over a ham which has been rubbed with dry mustard and ground cloves.

Quick Honey Fruit Dressing: Combine 3 tablespoons honey, ½ cup dairy sour cream, and a dash of mace.

Fruit Salad Dressing: Boil 1 minute ½ cup sugar, ½ cup honey, 1 tablespoon celery seed, 1 tablespoon dry mustard, 1 tablespoon paprika, ½ teaspoon salt, 2 tablespoons onion juice, and ¼ cup vinegar. Slowly add ½ cup vegetable oil. Store in covered jar in refrigerator. Makes about 1 pint. Bring to room temperature before serving.

Orange-Honey glaze for bundt or pound cake: Simmer ½ cup honey, ½ cup sugar, and ⅓ cup water for 5 minutes. Add 1 tablespoon orange juice concentrate; boil 2 minutes. Pour over cooled cake.

MUSHROOMS, CANNED

How to Use: Add to creamed and à la King dishes.

Add to casseroles.

Add to cooked vegetables such as peas, carrots, tomatoes, and green beans.

Sauté with sliced onions in butter until onions are golden. Serve with grilled steaks or hamburgers.

OLIVES

GREEN OLIVES

How to Use: Chop and add to dips, tossed vegetable salads, molded vegetable salads, and aspics.

Use for garnishes.

Use as for stuffed green olives.

STUFFED GREEN OLIVES

How to Use: Chop and mix with braunschweiger for a sandwich spread.

Slice and add to tuna-macaroni salad.

Steak sauce: Add chopped stuffed olives to ½ cup melted butter or margarine. Season with pepper and salt. Add minced parsley. Pour over broiled steak.

Olive Hamburger topping: Combine ⅓ cup sliced stuffed green olives, ⅓ cup sliced pitted ripe olives, 3 tablespoons mayonnaise, and 3 tablespoons dairy sour cream. Tops 6 hamburgers.

RIPE OLIVES

How to Use: Slice and toss with greens for a salad.

For a garnish, push a thin carrot stick through a pitted olive.

Chop and stir into cottage cheese along with diced green pepper and pimiento.

Mix with chipped beef, minced celery, and mayonnaise for a sandwich spread.

Blend chopped olives and chopped pecans with cream cheese for a sandwich filling.

Cover a lemon wedge with a lengthwise slice of ripe olive to use as garnish.

ORIENTAL VEGETABLES

BAMBOO SHOOTS

How to Use: Add to vegetable salads.

Substitute for celery in a variety of cooked dishes.

Add to noodle or macaroni casseroles for crispness and texture.

Add to vegetable soup.

Shred and add to egg foo yong or scrambled eggs.

Use in egg rolls, chop suey, or chow mein.

Dice and add to hamburger patties or meat loaf.

ORIENTAL VEGETABLE SOUP

3 *cups broth*
¼ *cup canned mushrooms, sliced*
⅓ *cup water chestnuts, sliced*
1 *cup fresh spinach or lettuce, shredded*
¼ *to* ⅓ *cup bamboo shoots, shredded*
½ *cup bean sprouts, if desired*

In medium saucepan heat broth to boiling. Add mushrooms, water chestnuts, spinach or lettuce, and bamboo shoots. Heat until warmed through. Just before serving add bean sprouts. Add salt or soy sauce to taste. Makes 4 cups soup.

BEAN SPROUTS

How to Use: Add to salads and sandwiches for crunchy texture.

Add to casseroles and soups during last few minutes of cooking or toss in just before serving.

Add to cooked vegetables during last 2 minutes of cooking.

Add to egg foo yong, fried rice, scrambled eggs, chop suey, chow mein, egg rolls, or Oriental stir-fry dishes.

Use as extender in hamburgers and meat loaf.

Green Beans and Bean Sprouts: Add sautéed chopped onions and soy sauce to cooked green beans. Heat until warmed through. Add bean sprouts just before serving. If desired, add sautéed mushroom slices also.

Stir fry chopped green pepper, onion, and bean sprouts; sprinkle with soy sauce before serving. Serve as accompaniment to broiled meats.

Add up to 1 cup chopped bean sprouts to 1 pound of ground beef for hamburger patties. Add ½ cup minced onion, 1 minced garlic clove, ¼ cup tomato juice or water, 2 tablespoons soy sauce, and basil to taste. Form into patties. Sauté or broil until meat is cooked.

Broiled Cheese-Sprout Sandwich: Toast bread on one side under broiler; turn over and top with a layer of bean sprouts and a hearty-flavored cheese. Or top bread with guacamole, tomato slices, bean sprouts, and cheese; broil until cheese is melted.

MEAT BALLS WITH ORIENTAL VEGETABLES

1 *pound ground beef*
1 *teaspoon salt*
⅛ *teaspoon pepper*
¼ *cup onion, chopped*
1 *clove garlic, minced*
¼ *to ½ cup bamboo shoots*
1 *cup celery, sliced on diagonal, or 1 cup water chestnuts, sliced*
1 *cup carrots, sliced on diagonal*
1 *cup beef broth*

1 *teaspoon ginger*
2 *tablespoons cornstarch*
1 *tablespoon soy sauce*
¼ *cup water*
2 *cups bean sprouts*
   Hot cooked rice

In medium bowl mix beef with salt and pepper. Shape into 1½-inch balls. In medium skillet with cover, brown meat; remove from pan. Add the garlic and onion; cook until tender. Drain excess drippings. Add bamboo shoots, celery or water chestnuts, carrots, and beef broth. Cover and cook until vegetables are tender, about 10 minutes. In small bowl, blend cornstarch, ginger, soy sauce, and water. Stir into vegetable mixture and cook until thickened. Add meat balls and heat until warmed through. Just before serving stir in bean sprouts. Serve over rice. Serves 2 to 4.

WATER CHESTNUTS

How to Use: Add thin slices to tossed salads and casseroles.
Add to fried rice or chop suey.
Substitute for celery in many recipes.
Use in Sukiyaki dishes.
Sauté in butter along with some sliced cashews or almonds; add with bean sprouts to cooked green beans.
Sauté in butter until lightly browned. Add to cooked green beans or peas. Season to taste with salt, pepper, and herbs.
Rumaki appetizers: Marinate water chestnuts in soy sauce and sugar for 30 minutes. Wrap with ⅓ of a slice of raw bacon and fasten with a wooden pick. Place on rack in broiler pan. Bake at 350° 30 to 35 minutes, or until bacon is crisp.

PIMIENTOS

How to Use: Add to creamed and à la King dishes for color appeal.
Add to cooked lima beans, peas, or corn.
Add to dips, cottage cheese, and scrambled eggs.

SOUPS (Canned Condensed)

CREAM SOUP (includes cream of chicken, cream of celery, and cream of mushroom)

How to Use: Combine with equal amounts of other canned soups. Add small amounts of cooked meats, cooked or raw vegetables, herbs and seasonings to taste. Dilute with milk, water, or broth.

Quick Corn Soup: Thin condensed cream soup with equal amount of milk. Add frozen or cooked corn. Heat and season to taste.

Use as a basting sauce for browned meat such as chicken, steaks, chops, or hamburger patties. Brown meat in vegetable oil; season to taste. Drain excess drippings. Stir in cream soup and dilute with water. Flavor with onion, herbs, or seasonings. Cover and simmer until meat is tender, or bake, covered, at 350° until meat is done.

Use as baking sauce for fish. *Sauce I:* Place ½ pound seasoned fish fillets in shallow greased baking dish. Combine ½ can condensed cream soup with a little dry white wine; pour over fish. Sprinkle with shredded cheese and paprika. Bake at 375° 45 minutes. *Sauce II:* Mix 1 can cream soup, grated cheese, salt, and pepper. Pour over fillets in greased baking dish. Mix 2 tablespoons bread crumbs and 1 tablespoon grated Parmesan cheese. Sprinkle over fish and sauce. Bake at 375° for 35 to 45 minutes.

Cream Soup Gravy: Remove fried or roasted meat from pan. Pour off drippings into a small container. Stir in condensed cream soup; stir well to loosen browned bits. Add a small amount of water and drippings. Heat, stirring frequently, until thick. If too thick, thin with water, milk, or broth to desired consistency.

Scalloped Vegetables: Place cooked vegetables in greased baking dish. Over them pour ½ can condensed cream soup seasoned to taste with onions, cheese, soy sauce, chopped nuts, and so on. Bake at 350° 20 to 30 minutes.

Use as a base for à la King dishes: Sauté green pepper in butter or vegetable oil. Add cream soup; thin to desired consistency with milk. Add pimiento and, if desired, a little dry sherry. Add chopped cooked chicken, turkey, or ham. Add cooked vegetables, if desired. Season to taste. Serve over toast, rice, noodles, or in baked squash shells.

Use as cream sauce: Sauté onion and celery in butter. Add cream soup and herbs or seasonings as desired. Serve over cooked meat or vegetables. Or add cooked chopped meat and cooked vegetables, thin with milk to desired consistency, and serve over muffins, biscuits, rice, noodles, or cooked potatoes.

TOMATO SOUP

How to Use: Combine with other soups such as green pea, vegetable, or beef noodle.

Quick Gazpacho: Combine tomato soup with an equal amount of water; add sliced cucumber, minced green pepper and onion, wine vinegar, minced garlic, and a dash of salt, pepper, and hot pepper sauce. Chill several hours.

Tomato Bouillon: Mix tomato soup with an equal amount of milk and 1 beef bouillon cube for each cup of liquid. Heat gently and serve.

Tomato-Corn Chowder: Combine condensed tomato soup with an equal amount of milk, a little sugar, and whole-kernel or cream-style corn. Heat until thoroughly warmed.

Use as sauce for cooking browned meat. Pour soup over meat; season with salt, pepper, onions, mushrooms, green pepper, and so on, as desired. Cover and cook over moderate heat until meat is tender.

Use as part of liquid in making meat loaf or patties of ground meat. Add up to ½ soup can to 1 pound of ground meat.

Add to cooking liquid when making stew or pot roast.

Barbecue sauce: Add to tomato soup some chopped onion and celery, minced garlic, brown sugar, vinegar, Worcestershire sauce, and prepared mustard. Simmer 10 minutes. Serve over meat loaf, spareribs, frankfurters, roasts, or chicken.

SWEET FRENCH DRESSING

½ (10¾-ounce) can condensed tomato soup
⅓ cup vinegar
¼ cup vegetable oil
1 small clove garlic, whole
⅓ cup sugar
1 teaspoon Worcestershire sauce
1½ teaspoons grated onion
½ teaspoon salt
½ teaspoon prepared mustard
½ teaspoon paprika

In pint jar with cover, combine all ingredients and shake well. Chill several hours before using.

Appendix

EQUIVALENT MEASURES
METRIC CONVERSIONS
FAHRENHEIT/CELSIUS CONVERSIONS
CANNED FOODS
COMMON FOOD EQUIVALENTS
SUBSTITUTIONS FOR COMMONLY USED FOODS
STORAGE GUIDE FOR PERISHABLE FOODS

Index

APPENDIX

EQUIVALENT MEASURES

A pinch or dash = less than ⅛
    teaspoon
3 teaspoons = 1 tablespoon
2 tablespoons = ⅛ cup
4 tablespoons = ¼ cup
5⅓ tablespoons = ⅓ cup
8 tablespoons = ½ cup

12 tablespoons = ¾ cup
16 tablespoons = 1 cup
1 cup = ½ pint
2 cups = 1 pint
2 pints = 1 quart
16 ounces = 1 pound
16 fluid ounces = 2 cups

APPROXIMATE COMPARISON OF CUSTOMARY AND METRIC VOLUME MEASURES *

CUSTOMARY	METRIC
1 quart	a little less than 1000 milliliters or 1 liter
1 cup	250 milliliters
½ cup	125 milliliters
1 tablespoon	15 milliliters
1 teaspoon	5 milliliters
½ teaspoon	2 milliliters

APPROXIMATE CONVERSION OF FAHRENHEIT TO CELSIUS TEMPERATURES

FAHRENHEIT	CELSIUS
300°F	150°C
325°F	160°C
350°F	180°C
375°F	190°C
400°F	200°C
425°F	220°C
450°F	230°C

Fahrenheit conversion to Celsius: $°F = (9/5 \times °C) + 32$
Celsius conversion to Fahrenheit: $°C = 5/9 \ (°F - 32)$

*Established by American National Standards Institute Subcommittee

CANNED FOODS

SIZE OF CAN	NUMBER OF CUPS
6 ounces	¾ cup
8 ounces	1 cup
10½ ounces	1¼ cups
12 ounces	1½ cups
15½ ounces	1¾ cups
16 ounces	2 cups
1 pound, 4 ounces	2½ cups
1 pound, 13 ounces	3½ cups
1 quart	4 cups
46 ounces	5¾ cups
6 pounds, 9 ounces	12 cups

COMMON FOOD EQUIVALENTS

Apples: 1 medium apple = 1 cup sliced
Banana: 1 medium banana = ½ cup mashed
Bread crumbs: 3 to 4 slices bread = 1 cup dry crumbs
               1 slice bread = ¾ cup soft crumbs
Butter: 1 pound = 2 cups
      ½ pound or 2 sticks = 1 cup
      ¼ pound (1 stick or 8 tablespoons) = ½ cup
      4 tablespoons or ½ stick = ¼ cup
      5⅓ tablespoons = ⅓ cup
Cabbage: 1 pound head = 4 cups shredded
Cheese: ¼ pound = 1 cup shredded
Cottage cheese: 8 ounces = 1 cup
Crackers, graham: 15 squares = 1 cup fine crumbs
Crackers, saltines: 16 squares = 1 cup coarse crumbs
                  22 squares = 1 cup fine crumbs
Cream cheese: 3 ounces = 6 tablespoons; 8 ounces = 1 cup
Cream, whipping: 1 cup unwhipped = 2 cups whipped
Dry beans: 1 cup = 2½ cups cooked
Milk, evaporated: 5⅓ fluid ounces = ⅔ cup; 13 fluid ounces = 1⅔ cups
Milk, sweetened condensed: 14 ounces = approximately 1⅓ cups
Noodles, macaroni and spaghetti: 8 ounces uncooked = 4 cups cooked
Onion: 1 medium = ½ cup chopped
      1 tablespoon instant dried onion = ¼ cup chopped raw onion
      ½ teaspoon onion powder = 1 tablespoon chopped raw onion
      1 teaspoon onion salt = flavor of 1 medium raw onion
Orange: 1 medium = ⅓ to ½ cup juice
Rice: 1 cup uncooked = 3 cups cooked
     1 cup precooked = 2 cups cooked

SUBSTITUTIONS FOR COMMONLY USED FOODS

INGREDIENT	QUANTITY	SUBSTITUTE
Baking powder	1 teaspoon	¼ teaspoon baking soda plus ⅝ teaspoon cream of tartar, OR ¼ teaspoon baking soda plus ½ cup buttermilk
Beef broth	1 cup	1 teaspoon beef-flavored concentrate or 1 beef bouillon cube dissolved in 1 cup boiling water
Biscuit mix	1 cup	1 cup flour, 1½ teaspoons baking powder, ½ teaspoon salt, 1 tablespoon shortening
Buttermilk	1 cup	1 tablespoon vinegar or lemon juice plus enough sweet milk to make 1 cup; let stand 5 minutes
Eggs	1 whole	2 egg yolks
Flour	1 tablespoon	½ tablespoon cornstarch or 2 teaspoons quick-cooking tapioca
Herbs	1 teaspoon dried	1 tablespoon fresh
Honey	1 cup	1¼ cups sugar plus ¼ cup liquid
Milk, whole	1 cup	½ cup evaporated milk plus ½ cup water
Mustard	1 tablespoon prepared	1 teaspoon dry mustard plus 1 tablespoon white wine or vinegar
Shortening, hydrogenated	1 cup	1⅛ cups butter or margarine, OR ⅞ cup oil plus ½ teaspoon salt
Sweetened condensed milk	1⅓ cups	1 cup plus 2 tablespoons instant nonfat dry milk plus ½ cup warm water and ¾ cup sugar: Place warm water in bowl, add dry milk and mix, then add sugar and mix until smooth; OR combine 2 eggs, 1 cup brown sugar, 1 teaspoon vanilla, 2 tablespoons flour, ½ teaspoon baking powder and ¼ teaspoon salt
Tomato paste	1 tablespoon	1 tablespoon tomato catsup
Tomato puree	1 cup	2 tablespoons tomato paste plus enough water to make 1 cup

STORAGE GUIDE FOR PERISHABLE FOODS

FOOD	STORAGE CONDITIONS		
	WHERE TO STORE	TYPE OF PACKAGING	USE WITHIN
Meat, Poultry, and Fish			
Cold cuts	Refrigerator*	Original wrapper or plastic wrap	If unopened up to 2 weeks If opened in 3 to 5 days
Frankfurters, bacon, smoked sausage	Refrigerator	Original wrapper or plastic wrap	1 week
Whole ham	Refrigerator	Original wrapper	1 week
Half ham	Refrigerator	Plastic wrap	5 days
Ham slices	Refrigerator	Plastic wrap	3 days
Fresh roasts, steaks, chops	Refrigerator	Plastic wrap	3 to 5 days
Bulk sausage	Refrigerator	Original wrapper or plastic wrap	3 to 4 days
Ground beef, pork, lamb	Refrigerator	Rewrap in plastic wrap	1 or 2 days
Poultry	Refrigerator	Original wrapper or plastic wrap	1 or 2 days
Fish	Refrigerator	Original wrapper	1 or 2 days
Liver, kidney, brains	Refrigerator	Original wrapper or plastic wrap	1 or 2 days
Poultry giblets	Refrigerator	Rewrap separately	1 or 2 days
Leftover cooked meat and meat dishes	Cool quickly, then refrigerate	Covered jars or plastic containers	3 or 4 days
Leftover stuffing from poultry	Remove from bird, cool at once, then refrigerate	Covered jars or plastic containers	1 or 2 days
Gravy	Refrigerator	Covered jar or plastic container	1 or 2 days
Meat broth	Refrigerator	Covered jar or plastic container	1 or 2 days
Milk, Cream, Cheese			
Fresh milk and cream	Refrigerator	Original container	1 week
Dry milk	Cupboard shelf	Tightly closed in original container	Several months
Evaporated milk, unopened	Cool dry place at temperature below 70°F.	Original container	Several months

* All refrigerator-storage recommendations are based on a maximum refrigerator temperature of 40°F. or 4°C.

Evaporated milk, opened	Refrigerator	Original container, covered	3 to 5 days
Sweetened condensed milk, unopened	Cool dry dark place	Original container	6 months
Sweetened condensed milk, opened	Refrigerator	Original container, covered	7 days
Buttermilk	Refrigerator	Original container	3 or 4 days or up to manufacturer's expiration date
Cheese, hard (cheddar, Parmesan, Swiss)	Refrigerator	Wrap tightly	Several months
Cheese, cottage	Refrigerator	Original container	3 to 5 days
Cheese, soft (cream, Camembert)	Refrigerator	Wrap tightly	2 weeks
Eggs			
Fresh in shell	Refrigerator	Original container	1 week
Raw yolks	Refrigerator	Cover with cold water, in covered container	2 to 4 days
Raw whites	Refrigerator	Covered container	2 to 4 days
Vegetables			
Asparagus	Refrigerator crisper	Unwashed in plastic bag	2 or 3 days
Broccoli, Brussels sprouts	Refrigerator crisper	Plastic bag or wrap	3 to 5 days
Cauliflower, celery	Refrigerator crisper	Plastic bag or wrap	1 week
Cabbage	Refrigerator crisper	Plastic bag or wrap	2 weeks
Green beans	Refrigerator crisper	Plastic bag or wrap	1 week
Carrots, beets, radishes, turnips, parsnips	Refrigerator	Remove tops, store in plastic bag or wrap	2 weeks
Green peas, lima beans	Refrigerator	Leave in pods	3 to 5 days
Lettuce, salad greens	Refrigerator crisper	Wash and drain, place in plastic bag or wrap	1 week
Onions, dry	Room temperature	Mesh or loosely woven container	Several months
Onions, green	Refrigerator crisper	Plastic bag or wrap	3 to 5 days
Peppers, cucumbers	Refrigerator crisper	Wash, dry, place in plastic wrap or bag	1 week
Potatoes	Dark dry place with good ventilation, 45° to 50°F.		Several months; if storing at room temperature, within 3 to 5 days

Spinach, kale, collards, chard, beet, turnip, and mustard greens	Refrigerator crisper	Wash and drain well, place in plastic wrap	3 to 5 days
Squash, summer	Refrigerator crisper	Plastic wrap	3 to 5 days
Squash, winter	Dry place, 60°F.	Unwrapped	Several months
Sweet potato, eggplant, rutabaga	Dry place, 60°F.	Unwrapped	Several months; if stored at room temperature, within 1 week
Tomatoes, ripe	Refrigerator	Unwrapped	Up to 1 week
Tomatoes, unripe	Room temperature, away from sunlight	Unwrapped	When ripened
Vegetables, cooked	Refrigerator	Covered container	1 to 3 days

Fruit

Handle all fruits carefully to prevent bruising. Sort out bruised or decaying fruit before storing.

Apples, ripe	Refrigerator	Plastic bag	1 month
Apples, unripe	60° to 70°F.	Plastic bag with damp towel	Several months
Apricots, nectarines, peaches, plums, ripe	Refrigerator	Unwrapped	3 to 5 days; if unripe, store at room temperature until ripened
Avocados, bananas, pears, unripe	Room temperature	Unwrapped	Until ripened
Avocados, bananas, pears, ripe	Refrigerator	Unwrapped	3 to 5 days
Berries	Refrigerator	Unwashed in covered container	2 or 3 days
Cherries	Refrigerator	Unwashed, stems on, covered container	2 or 3 days
Cranberries	Refrigerator	Covered container	1 week
Grapes	Refrigerator	Covered lightly	3 to 5 days
Citrus fruits	60° to 70°F. or refrigerator	Uncovered	2 weeks
Melons, unripe	Room temperature	Uncovered	Until ripened
Melons, ripe	Refrigerator	Covered, if cut	2 or 3 days
Pineapple, fresh uncut	Room temperature	Uncovered	As soon as possible
Pineapple, fresh cut	Refrigerator	Covered	2 or 3 days
Rhubarb	Refrigerator	Plastic wrap	3 to 5 days
Canned fruits and fruit juice	Refrigerator	Covered container	3 or 4 days

INDEX

Entries in FULL CAPITALS indicate perishable food items; entries with Initial Capitals refer to specific categories such as Salads, Desserts, etc.; *Recipe Titles* are given in italics.